HILLWALKING LONDON

Caroline Buckland has worked for her entire career
in the publishing and media industries.
An avid walker, she lives in south-east London.

HILLWALKING LONDON

Caroline Buckland

SAFE HAVEN

To Peter and Audrey

Acknowledgements

Graham Coster – 'the boss' – without whom this book would not exist, and for his wise counsel and company on many a ramble.

Steven Bode – for patiently reading my prose and accompanying me on the journey.

Ian Buckland – for suggesting the Guinness Hills.

Vincent Lacovara, Ian Sampson, Melanie Sharp, and Helena Clarkson and Caroline Benson of the Museum of English Rural Life at the University of Reading.

Anyone who's ever been on a walk with me.

First published 2023 by Safe Haven Books Ltd
12 Chinnocks Wharf
14 Narrow Street
London E14 8DJ
www.safehavenbooks.co.uk

Text copyright © Caroline Buckland 2023

The moral right of Caroline Buckland to be identified as the Author of the text of this work has been asserted by her in accordance with the Copyrights, Designs and Patents Act, 1988.

All Rights Reserved. No part of this book may reproduced or utilised in any form or by any means, electronic or mechanical, including photocopying, recording or by any information storage and retrieval system, without permission in writing from Safe Haven Books Ltd.

Every effort has been made to contact the copyright holders of material in this book. Where an omission has occurred, the publisher will gladly include acknowledgement in any future edition.

A catalogue record for this book is available from the British Library.

ISBN 978 1 8384051 7 5

10 9 8 7 6 5 4 3 2 1

The Safe Haven team on *Hillwalking London*: Caroline Buckland, Graham Coster, Tim Peters and David Welch

Maps: OS Open Map - Local

Designed and typeset in Gill Sans and Tablet Gothic Semi-Condensed by TimPetersDesign.co.uk

Printed and bound in the EU by GraphyCems

MIX
Paper from responsible sources
FSC® C007507

Picture Credits

All pictures by Graham Coster except:

Caroline Buckland: 2–3, 27 (top), 63 (bottom), 64 (bottom), 74–5, 76, 81 (top), 84 (bottom), 87 (bottom), 88, 89 (right)

Alamy: 15 (bottom), 20 (top), 22 (top), 34 (bottom), 56 (bottom), 60, 67, 81 (bottom), 86, 101, 112, 130, 150–51, 153

Chris Ellis: 17 (bottom)

Hornsey Historical Society: 18 (bottom)

London Natural History Society: 24

Vestry House Museum: 31 (bottom)

Sewardstone Park Cemetery: 37

Niles Crane, Flickr: 47

Wikicommons: 54 (bottom), 89 (left), 136 (bottom), 139

Pierre Terre, Geograph 55 (top)

Reg Bickersdyke: 56 (top), 57 (middle and bottom)

Geograph: 79 (bottom left)

Tim Peters: 55 (bottom), 87 (top and middle)

MICA: 93 (bottom)

Mathew Frith: 102

Paul Lawrence, Long Distance Walkers Association: 104 (top)

Look & Learn: 104 (bottom)

Paul (Bangkok Bloke), Flickr: 105 (bottom)

Museum of Rural Life, University of Reading; Clifford Tandy Collection: 118 (top)

Architectural Press Archive/RIBA: 118 (bottom)

© Historic England Archive. Aerofilms Collection: 138

Timku, Flickr: 142

Subterranea Britannica: 155 (bottom)

Contents

5 *Acknowledgements and Picture Credits*

8–9 *Greater London Map*

10 *Introduction*

13 **A Highgate Highline** – Alexandra Palace to Archway

24 *The Geography and Geology of London*

29 **Reservoir Jogs** – Chingford and the Sewardstone Hills

41 **Five Parks Rising to a Peak** – Romford to Havering Park

52 *London's 20 Highest Hills*

53 Whitechapel Mount

54 The Hills of the City of London

56 Beckton Alps

58 Stave Hill

61 **Three Rivers and Four Hills (including Octavia)**
 – Brockley to Greenwich

74 Shooters Hill

77 **Telegraphs, Beacons and Masts** – New Cross Gate to Forest Hill

88 Crystal Palace

91 **Seven Hills of Croydon** – East Croydon to New Addington

104 *Water Towers*

107 **A Royal Park and a Commoner Common**
 – Richmond to Wimbledon

118 The Guinness Hills

119 Primrose Hill

121 **Hills Ancient and Modern** – Perivale to Northolt

133 **Country and North-Western** – Stanmore to Harrow Weald

144 *Trig Points*

147 **High on the Heath** – Hampstead Heath to Golders Green

160 *Bibliography and Useful Web Addresses*

Greater London Map

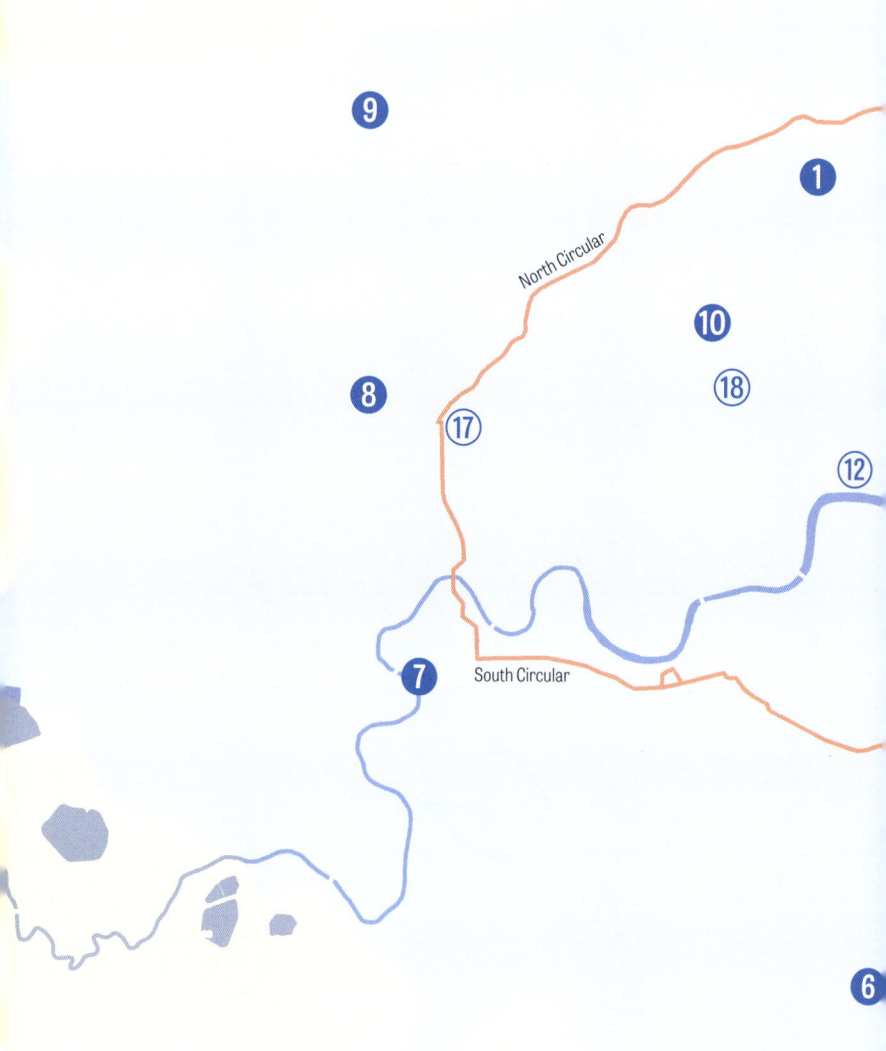

North Circular

South Circular

The numbers show the locations of the walks and hills that follow.

1 walk

11 single hill

Greater London Map 9

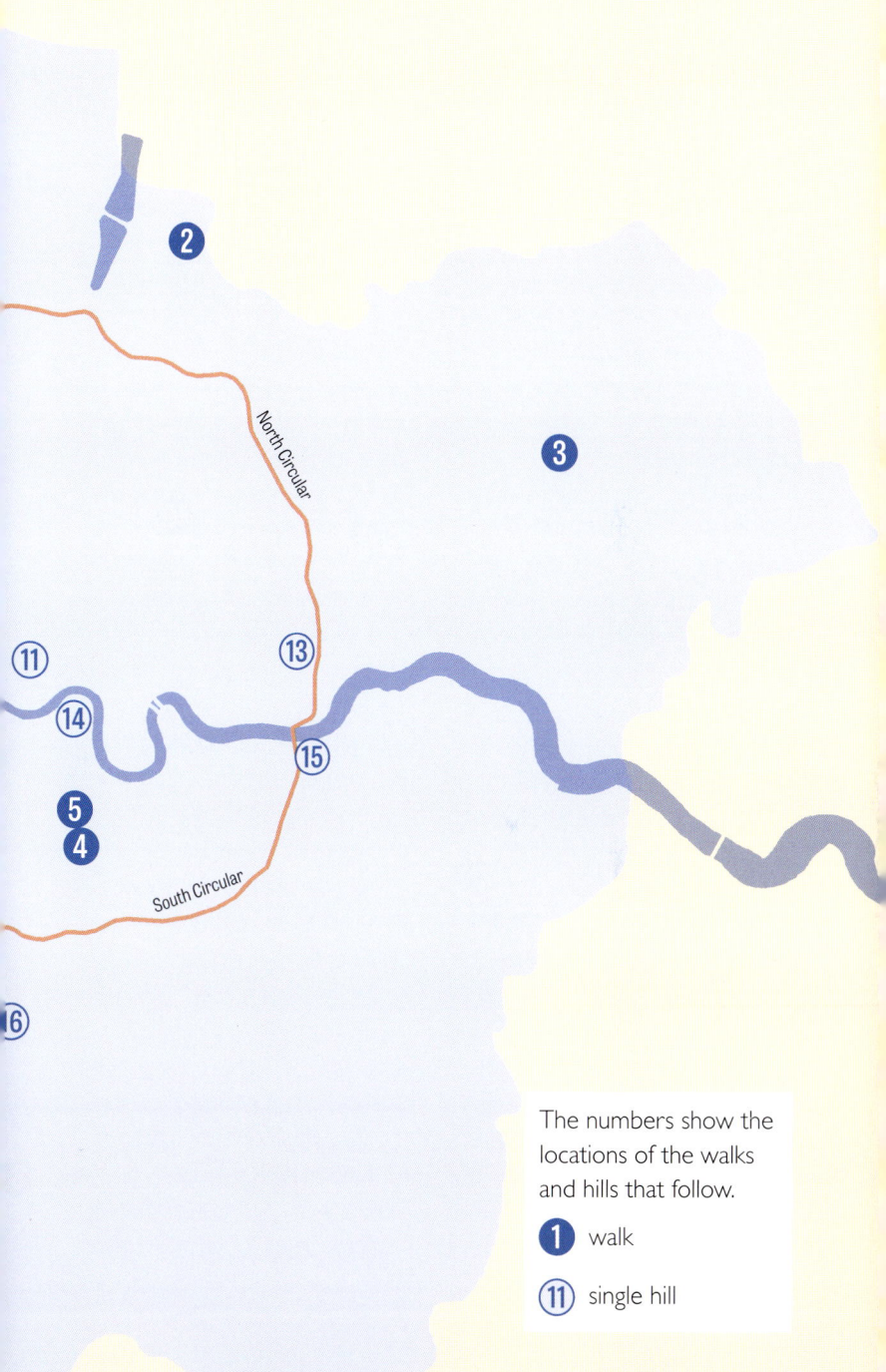

Introduction

London is a city bursting with hills. It may not have the mythological romance of Rome and its seven hills, but most boroughs have their fair share of them, and this topography has played a major role in the capital's evolution. Not all world cities have followed the same trajectory: Manhattan's hills were deliberately flattened to accommodate its neat grid pattern.

This book bounced into life during a bracing lockdown walk in Greenwich Park. While marvelling at what I still think the most majestic panorama in London – from the Royal Observatory viewpoint – my companion and I found ourselves pondering the park's more ancient history (Saxon burial mounds towards its western edge), and wondering how far you could join up a walk to the surrounding hills.

As soon as the restriction to local haunts was lifted, a plan was hatched: to seek out more views, walk some of the highest hills all around London, and see if we could find enough arresting walks to fill a whole volume. The book you hold represents that voyage of discovery.

Why walk up a hill? For the chest-pumping, butt-firming exercise. For the calming and contemplative experience of being at one with your surroundings. And for the promise of a unique and stunning view – in this case to remind us what a truly beautiful city we live in.

Not every London peak is included. I have avoided borrowing too heavily from well-established routes like the London Loop and Capital Ring, and commend them for further explorations – Crystal Palace, for example, is on a fine section of the Green Chain Walk. Some of London's highest points also turn out to be only accessible via busy roads, too far from frequent public transport, or simply lack any views at all.

I have also included discrete hills that don't fall on any obvious walking route, and the most interesting examples of that strange phenomenon, the artificial hill, extant and vanished, which can provide prospects of the capital to rival any natural eminence.

These walks are only possible today because London's citizens took steps to protect the land and its precious views. Mid-nineteenth-century urbanisation saw access to green space being seen as a public right, and the opening up of once private royal parklands such as Richmond Park, and new large public parks, like Bedford Park in Havering.

More land came from historic estates, through either the philanthropy of social reformers or crippling death duties, with only the name surviving of the now-vanished estate or benefactor, as at Golders Hill

The descent from Pembroke Lodge, Richmond Park, to Petersham Meadows.

Park or Croydon's Lloyd Park.

Meanwhile, direct action was mobilised to defend common land against encroaching development. From up to 10,000 demonstrators protecting One Tree Hill against a proposed golf course, to the river crossing scheme threatening Oxleas Wood and Shooters Hill in the 1990s, the power of the people, as individuals and groups like the Commons Preservation Society, preserved many of the heaths and commons we visit.

These ten walks are designed as leisurely excursions for the serious and non-serious walker alike. Hiking boots are not necessary, but more rural sections may be muddy. Binoculars are recommended. Timings allow for breaks and admiring views, but for maximum enjoyment most walks require the best part of a day. I have indicated points where those short of time or energy can cut the expedition short.

A decent walk deserves the reward of refreshment, whether a kickstart coffee, afternoon tea and cake, or even lunch, so suggestions for Base Camp are provided. A striking location only adds to the pleasure.

Views change with the seasons: leaves fall to expose hidden views, while progress sees ever more skyscrapers clutter the horizon. Every one of these walks reveals unexpected vistas, histories and narratives of how London has been shaped by its hills. Certainly our ancestors appreciated their strategic advantages for scanning the surrounding terrain or defending a settlement. So perhaps it's a primal response to head for the hills.

The television mast at the top of Alexandra Park.

❶
A Highgate Highline
Alexandra Palace to Archway

Though this feels like a mostly downhill walk from the early peak of Alexandra Palace – one of the most exhilarating and panoramic prospects of the metropolis to be had anywhere in Greater London – in fact it takes you higher still, reaching its zenith shortly before Highgate Village via more arresting views. It winds its way back down to the traffic hub of Archway via a picturesque route of old railway line, ancient woodland and one of London's most elegant parks, with a peek at one of the world's most famous cemeteries. The route can be reversed for a slightly more challenging walk.

Summits:
Alexandra Palace, 89m
Muswell Hill, 105m – 17th highest point in London
North Hill, Highgate, 136m – 10th highest point in London
Highgate Wood, 101m

Length: 4 miles – 6.5 km
Time: 2½ hours (timings uphill may vary depending on fitness levels)
Total ascent: 453 feet – 138 metres
Start: Alexandra Palace Station (Great Northern line from Moorgate). Wood Green Station on the Piccadilly Line is also in walking distance.
Finish: Archway Station (Northern Line)
Base camp: Coffee shop at Alexandra Palace Station. Many opportunities for refreshments along the way: e.g. Alexandra Park, Highgate Wood and Waterlow Park. Shops in Highgate Village.
• Visits to Highgate Cemetery may need to be booked in advance (check restrictions). There is also an entrance fee. highgatecemetery.org

---

Opposite Alexandra Park Station on St Michael's Terrace is the Starting Gate pub, a reference to Alexandra Park's racecourse (see inset box).

Turn left out of the station and left again over the footbridge across the railway. Cross the road at the pedestrian crossing and turn left to go through the

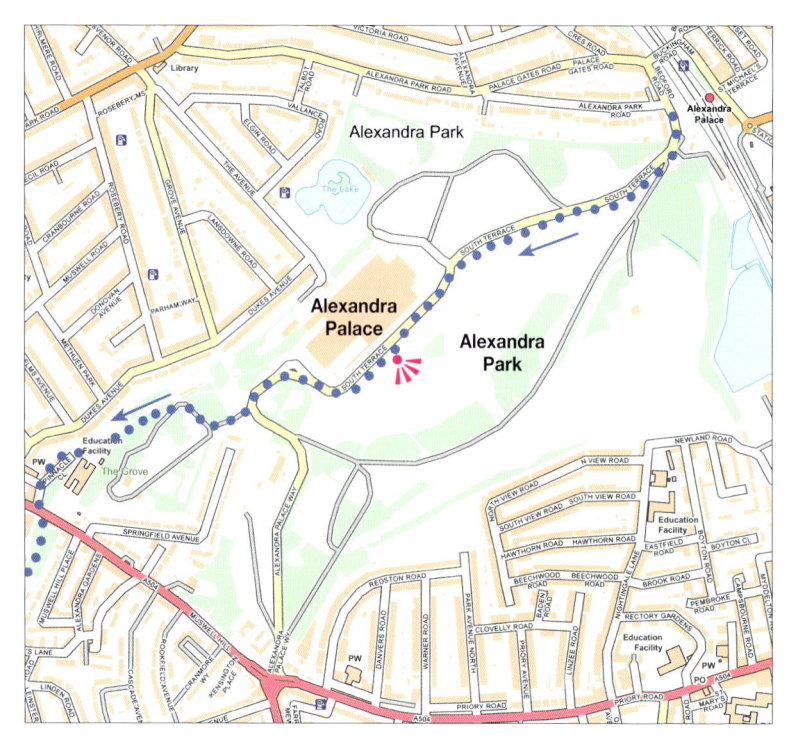

14 A Highgate Highline

gate to Alexandra Park. This is gate 2, and you will be aiming for gate 9 as detailed on the park map.

Follow the path uphill through the park, running broadly parallel to the road on your left. As you climb you'll get progressively better views of the Shard, the City and Canary Wharf. Turn right and then left upwards in the direction of the TV tower ahead. Look back in the direction you've just come and across to the north-east you'll see the spaceship-like presence

Alexandra Park

The 80 sloping acres of Alexandra Park were laid out in 1863 out on the site of the ancient Tottenham Wood, part of the Great Forest of Middlesex. Incorporated within it was Alexandra Park's racecourse, opened in 1868 and known colloquially on account of its shape as 'the Frying Pan'. It was the only course within London, and closed as late as 1970, but was hated by jockeys like Willie Carson for its notoriously sharp and slippery bends. Its course can still be clearly traced down at the bottom of the park. The park's cricket ground is probably unique for having been sited in the centre of the course and having been reached via a footbridge over it.

Alexandra Palace to Archway 15

The Tottenham Hotspur Stadium in the distance, from the terrace in Alexandra Park.

of the new Tottenham Hotspur Stadium. Make your way through the gardens and the car park towards the main terrace at the front of Alexandra Palace.

From the terrace, stupendous views of London spread out, from Canary Wharf and Docklands across the City and St Paul's, and over to the Crystal Palace transmitter on the distant southern hills.

Alexandra Palace

Alexandra Palace was never a palace. It was built in 1863 to be a theatre, entertainment venue and ice rink, and named after the new Princess of Wales, wife of the future Edward VII. A mere 16 days after its grand opening it was destroyed by fire. (This will become a theme.) Two years later it had been rebuilt, this time its grounds incorporating everything from a racecourse to a theatre, a boating lake, a circus and a concert hall.

But Ally Pally has continued to have a chequered history – in 1980 another serious fire caused major structural damage, and it reopened in 1988 after reconstruction work. By 1900 an Act of Parliament saw it become publicly owned, and during the First World War it was first used to house refugees from Belgium and Netherlands, and later became an internment camp for 17,000 German, Austrian and Hungarian civilians. The Second World War saw it again house refugees, as well as serving as a staging area for troops returning from Dunkirk.

It's most famous for its association with the birth of BBC television, the arrival of the iconic transmitter mast in 1935 heralding the inaugural high-definition TV service broadcast the following year. BBC News had its studios there from 1954 until 1969.

Ally Pally's Great Hall has hosted musical events ranging from the 1968 legendary 14-hour Technicolor Dream featuring Pink Floyd to today's major rock, rap and pop acts, and in recent years has become the atmospheric venue for sporting fixtures like snooker's Masters Championship and, over Christmas and New Year, the raucous PDC World Darts Championship, when the place is invaded by fancy-dressed hordes got up as anything from Vikings to Elvis. Its historic theatre was finally reopened in 2018.

Richard Baker reads the news at the BBC TV studios at Alexandra Palace

To the west you can see the green cupola of St Michael's Church, Highgate. At the far end of the terrace refreshments are available at the Phoenix Bar and Kitchen.

When you've taken in enough of the view, pass the Palm Court entrance and head down to take path to the right. You'll pass a bridge on your right – this carried the railway that used to run up to Alexandra Palace (see the inset box on the Parkland Walk). At the signpost follow the path to Meeson House. Continue uphill and you'll find yourself at the Grove Café, a popular spot serving up drinks, sandwiches and ice cream from Wednesday to Sunday – and, if you're lucky, Italian arias sung by the cheerful patron!

Continue on the path beyond the café

The Parkland Walk from Alexandra Palace along the old railway line.

to the park's exit 9. Take the path ahead of you under the road to Parkland Walk

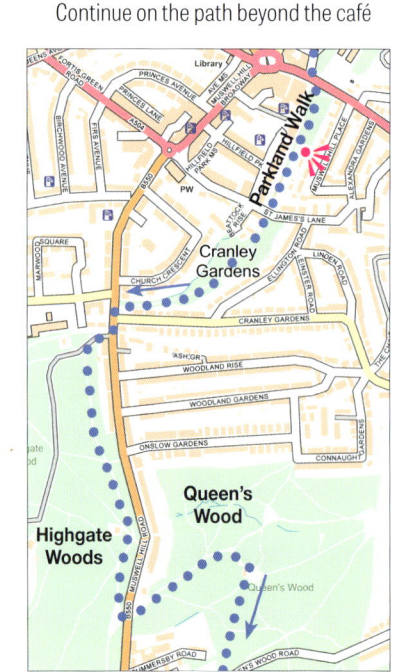

Parkland Walk

The Parkland Walk follows the course of the Edgware, Highgate and London Railway's branch line which opened in 1873 to connect Alexandra Palace with Finsbury Park. The train service ended in 1957, but the trackbed reopened as a park in 1984, and at 4km in length is the longest linear nature reserve in London.

18 A Highgate Highline

Continue through the wood and pass under the road bridge and up some steps into Cranley Gardens (try not to think of Dennis Nilsen, the serial killer who lived on this road). Turn left, then right into Highgate Woods through Cranley Gate opposite the traffic lights. If you fancy a quick trip into Muswell Hill Village then, instead of turning left at the top of the steps, turn right and follow Muswell Hill North, and follow this onto the trackbed of the disused railway line we encountered earlier, which has been repurposed as a wonderful parkland walk extending all the way to Finsbury Park.

This Muswell Hill section of the walk follows the southern flank of Muswell Hill itself and delivers spectacular views from atop the 17-arch viaduct. To the left the City and Docklands are visible, with Shooters Hill behind. Further round in the east you can see the tangled geometry of the Mittal tower in the Olympic Park at Stratford, and beyond that the tower blocks of Ilford and the hills of Loughton and Essex. If you subsequently walk the Chingford and Sewardstone Hills walk (p. 29) you'll find yourself looking back from those same hills at Alexandra Palace. To the right is the spire of St James's Church, Muswell Hill.

Among the beech trees in Highgate Woods.

Road; it's not very far. The highest point is on Fortis Green Road.

Formerly owned by the Bishops of London as their hunting grounds, Highgate Woods are part of the ancient forest of Middlesex. More prosaically, gravel pits were dug in them for the surfacing of

Alexandra Palace to Archway

The sylvan cricket ground in Highgate Woods.

local roads, before the woods were acquired in the nineteenth century by their present owner, the City of London.

Follow the signpost to 'Café and Playground', which takes you uphill through a lovely beech grove. When you reach the sign that offers you a choice of café or playground, go for 'Playground' to take you towards New Gate, which will be your point of exit from the woods.

The café is situated in an old cricket pavilion and looks out over a cricket

The Queen's Wood Café.

ground so bucolic and sylvan it could be in the heart of the Surrey Hills. It's still used by a couple of cricket clubs. A great place for a pitstop, the café is open seven days a week from 8 a.m. to 4.00 p.m. There are toilets here too. If you visit the café, just retrace your steps to the signpost and head towards the playground and you will see New Gate on your left.

Beyond the gate you will see the entrance to Queen's Wood opposite. Cross

Mary Kingsley

Kingsley Place is named after the eminent Victorian ethnographer, writer and explorer of Africa, Mary Kingsley, and a little further along Southwood Lane at number 22 is her house (complete with blue plaque). One of the first Western women to travel independently in Africa, she made two expeditions to the west coast in 1893 and 1894, exploring Sierra Leone, Angola and Gabon, and becoming the first to climb a new route up Mount Cameroon. Three previously unknown species of fish she discovered during a canoeing trip are named after her.

Travels in West Africa, her classic account of these amazingly intrepid solo expeditions, became an immediate bestseller on publication in 1897 and is still deservedly in print as a Penguin Classic. Mary Kingsley died in Cape Town in 1900 of typhoid, having volunteered to nurse during the second Boer War.

---

the road and enter the wood. Immediately to your left is the Queen's Wood Café (temporarily closed at the time of writing but hopefully not for long) and Organic Garden, a lovely spot for a rest among the vegetable and flower beds.

After the café take the lower path to the right down through the woods, then the path uphill towards Queenswood Road. Turn right onto the semi-rural Queenswood Road where it becomes Wood Lane, which transforms into a smart residential road. Continue to the traffic lights with the main road; down to your left is Highgate Station on the Northern Line, where you can truncate your walk if you wish.

At the lights cross over to Southwood Lane opposite and begin the climb towards Highgate Village. North Hill, the highest point in Highgate, runs parallel with Southwood Lane. On the left-hand side at the junction with Kingsley Place you'll be rewarded with sweeping views to the east of London, including in the distance the hills of Essex.

At the junction with Highgate High Street turn left into Highgate Village, a cornucopia of eateries, pubs and shops. Walk down the hill (more views out over London) until you come to the traffic lights and crossing outside the Côte brasserie. Cross the road here and enter Waterlow Park opposite.

Take the path to your right downhill until you reach two lakes. If you want to visit Highgate Cemetery, carry on to Swain's Lane Lodge Gate. Alternatively, once you're past the lakes, take the path to your left back uphill. Even if you don't want to take a formal tour of the cemetery or even pay to go inside, you can still take

Waterlow Park

This 26-acre park is set on a steep hillside landscaped to provide stunning views over the city. The land was donated by Sir Sydney Waterlow to be a 'garden for the gardenless', and the park opened in 1891.

Sir Sydney Waterlow had worked in his family's printing business before becoming a liberal politician known for his philanthropic works such as building housing for the poor. An MP for two Kent constituencies, he became Lord Mayor of London in 1872, and is commemorated with a statue at the top of the park. His former home, Lauderdale House, and its formal terraced gardens are also incorporated into the park.

The park is something of a hidden treasure, and a lovely place to explore in its own right. For our purposes it offers a scenic route down to Archway Station (via Lower Dartmouth Park Hill Gate), and it's also the way, via Swain's Lane Gate, to Highgate Cemetery.

On entering the park keep to your left, where you'll come upon Sir Sidney Waterlow's statue set back among the benches and trees. Immediately in front of him, beyond the gorgeous slopes of

Sir Sydney Waterlow's statue.

The Shard visible above the trees from Waterlow Park.

22 A Highgate Highline

greensward, there are views over the City and, depending on tree cover, even the dome of St Paul's Cathedral. Follow the path round and to the left are the formal gardens and terraces of Lauderdale House, today an arts and education centre with a nice café. Poking through the trees you'll see the green cupola of St Joseph's Church.

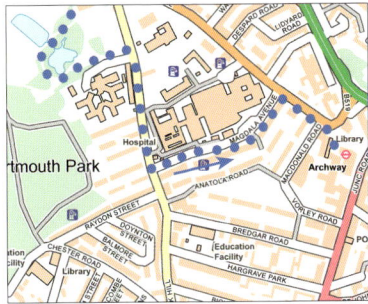

a peek: on your right-hand side, you can peer through the fence and, if you keep your eyes peeled you'll be able to make out the leonine features of Karl Marx on his substantial gravestone.

When you reach Lower Dartmouth Park Hill Gate, turn right down Dartmouth Park Hill past the Whittington Hospital and, on your right, the Whittington Estate, a brutalist gem from the 1970s designed by Peter Tabori.

The Whittington Estate.

Turn left into Magdala Avenue, and continue along it till it joins Highgate Hill. Turn right to find Archway Station on your right.

Alexandra Palace to Archway 23

The Geography and Geology of London

Why is London so hilly?

That the capital is surrounded by hills, a series of ridges and hill ranges stretching out across Greater London, to an extent we might imagine it as one giant amphitheatre with the Thames at its centre, is down to millions of years of geological activity.

Sometimes this was turbulent, the landscape periodically folding and fracturing as it was pushed up or depressed by tectonic movements. At other times it evolved over aeons literally grain by grain of sand through the natural action of water, either as sea levels rose or fell to deposit layers of sedimentary chalks, clays and gravels, or as rivers scoured out a valley to leave higher ground either side.

Another term for London's natural amphitheatre would be a basin, and indeed the modern metropolis of London sits within the London Basin. Over 65 million years ago, in the Cretaceous period, sea levels rose and warm seas flooded what is now southern England; what built up on the sea bed was ultimately left behind as a basin-like layer of chalk.

During the later Eocene epoch, a mere 56–34 million years ago, more sea-bed sediment was slowly piled up on top of that chalk. This was London Clay, which in some places is 150 metres deep. And on top of this lie the gravel and sands unique to particular areas and geological periods.

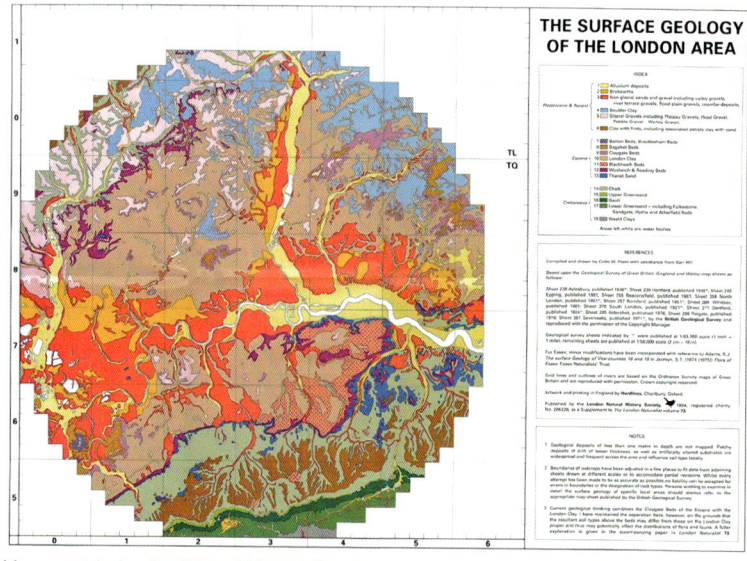

Map copyright London Natural History Society; cartography by Colin W. Plant.

Every single particle of it was created, and then deposited somewhere, by the ceaseless, erosive motion of water.

More recently (though we're still talking millions of years), the mighty River Thames has played an instrumental role in the creation of many of the hills in this book, especially in the north-west and south-west of London. Once upon a time it travelled a more northerly route, through what is now Hertfordshire, but successive Richmond Park and Wimbledon Common. The hills that rise up from the river in the City – Ludgate, Cornhill and Tower Hill, and indeed the rest of central London – are also composed from the accumulation of river gravel deposits.

In north-west London the presence of Stanmore Gravel in the composition of the ridge of Harrow Weald and Stanmore also dates it back to a time before the Thames changed course more than 2

The Thames below Richmond Hill.

ice ages beginning 2.5 million years ago gradually pushed the river south, to its current course, eroding the clay as it went and creating a series of sand and gravel terraces from glacial debris, which formed hills.

For example, the river carved out the bluff that would become Richmond Hill, but also deposited Black Park Gravel, one of the oldest river terraces, dating from the retreat of the Anglian Ice Sheet 400,000 years ago, to create what is now million years ago. At Horsenden Hill the clay is topped with Dollis Hill Gravel, a river terrace deposit from a tributary of the Thames that may once have stretched from the Weald of Kent prior to the river's diversion.

At Havering-atte-Bower on the north-east edge of London an outcrop of pebble gravel is found, which may be from another northward-flowing tributary, an attribute it shares with Shooters Hill in south-east London.

To the immediate north of the city the river's influence is evident in a series of ridges created by sand and gravel terraces which often dominate the surroundings. The highest takes in Hampstead Heath and Highgate, then continues eastwards to Crouch Hill and Queen's Wood, and age gravels that runs from Muswell Hill through to Whetstone in the north and Alexandra Palace in the east.

To the east, Pole Hill in the Sewardstone Hills consists of clay capped with Claygate Beds – alternating layers of sand and loam that were deposited on the

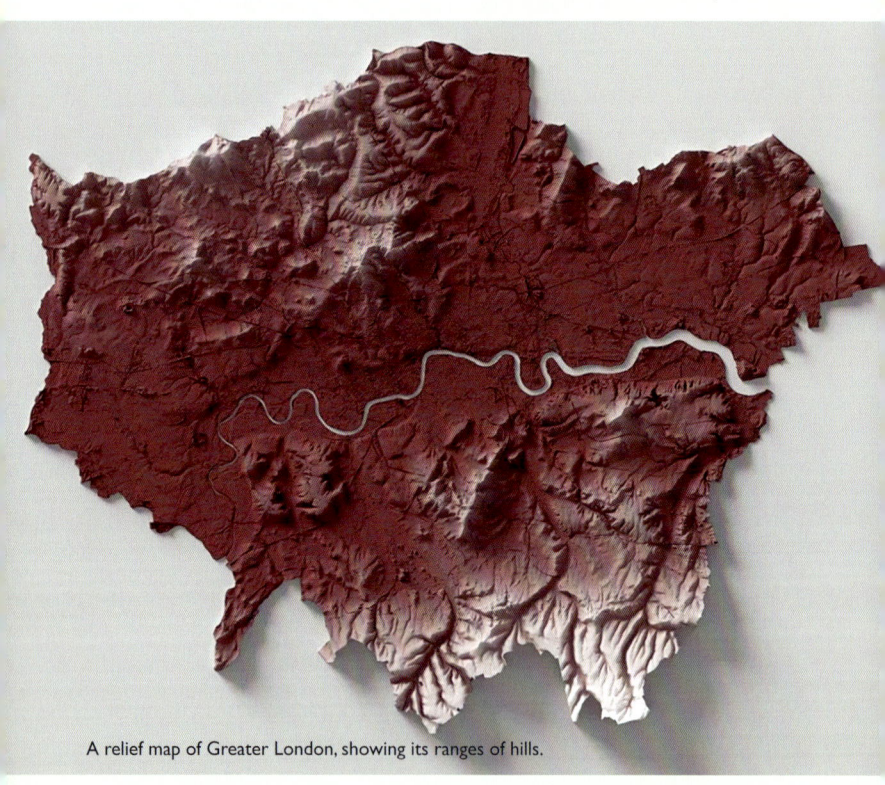

A relief map of Greater London, showing its ranges of hills.

immediately south to Parliament Hill and Primrose Hill. A smaller outlier of this ridge is Harrow. These hills are formed by the Bagshot Beds – sands that date back to the shallow waters of the pre-glacial age that sit atop the clay. Further north lies a second lower ridge of younger, glacial- floor of a shallow, subtropical sea.

Just south of the Thames ridges bestride the landscape. One forms Shooters Hill, Blackheath and Greenwich Park, and then goes on southwards to form Telegraph Hill, Nunhead, Honor Oak and Denmark Hill. Yet another further

Blackheath gravel from the pre-glacial age.

south forms Sydenham Hill and Crystal Palace. These are the heartlands of London Clay, interspersed with deposits of Blackheath and Woolwich Beds marine gravels from the pre-glacial age.

Other rivers besides the Thames are responsible for some of the hills we encounter on the walks in this book. At Lewisham, for example, the Shooters Hill-to-Crystal Palace ridge is punctuated by the Ravensbourne river valley cutting through, while the plateau of Richmond Park is divided from Wimbledon Common by the Beverley Brook eroding a course between them.

On the far southern edge of Greater London, Croydon lies on a different formation of high ground: the much older chalk backslopes of the North Downs, overlaid with Blackheath and Woolwich Beds.

The sandy soil evident on this path across Richmond Park.

King George's Reservoir from Barn Hill.

❷

Reservoir Jogs

Chingford and the Sewardstone Hills

This walk, from the end of the Overground line from Liverpool Street, climbs quickly out of Chingford up onto the range of compact summits that form the Sewardstone Hills stretching over the Greater London boundary into Essex to touch the edge of Epping Forest. From the three hilltops there are sweeping views out over the chain of reservoirs along the Lee Valley, and along the way unexpected landmarks to those enigmatic Edwardians Baden-Powell and Lawrence of Arabia.

Summits:
Pole Hill, 92m
Yardley Hill, 67m
Barn Hill, 60m

Length: 6 miles – 9.5 km
Time: 3 hours
Total ascent: 562 feet – 171 metres
Start and finish: Chingford Station – Overground
Base camp: Cafés up Station Road in Chingford town centre. (There are no refreshment or toilet options along the walk itself).

The walk starts at Connaught Avenue opposite the station, which we follow uphill to its end before taking the path ahead up into woods. Follow it until it opens out into a grassy clearing. This is the summit of Pole Hill, and the walk's highest point – remarkable how quickly we have left behind the solid semis and chunky SUVs of suburbia to find ourselves high among tranquil woodland.

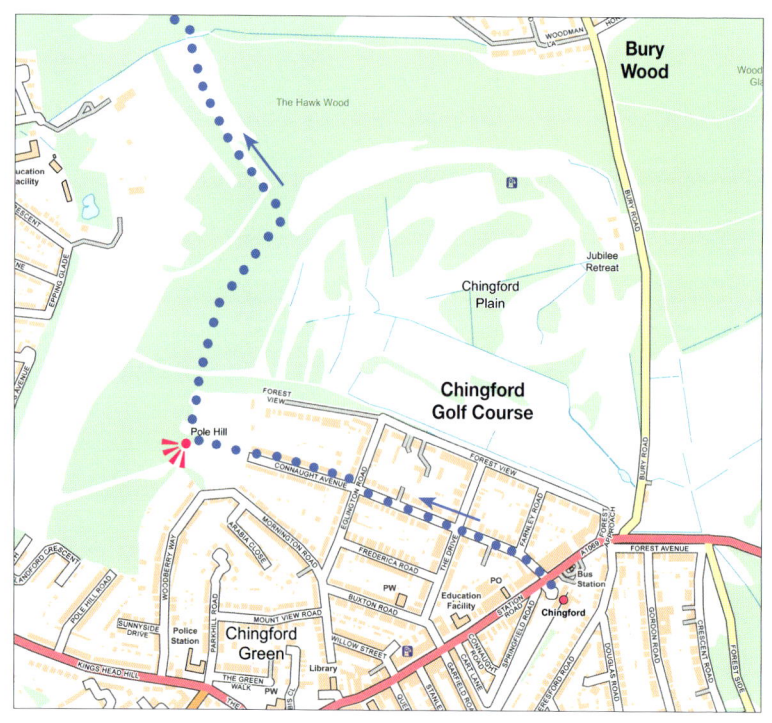

There's a bench at the summit perfectly placed to enjoy the view of King George's Reservoir, William Girling Reservoir and the Lee Valley Park, the vast stretches of water part of the Lee Valley chain that comprises 13 separate reservoirs supplying drinking water to north London. In the distance you can see the City and the BT Tower. From a green just to the left of the bench the view takes in Long Hills, Epping Forest and the green spire of Chingford United Reformed Church, as well as the Landmark Tower (an old water tower) in Repton Park.

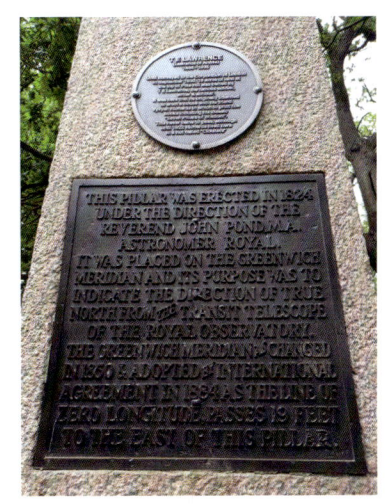

Pole Hill is also graced by a trig point (see p. 144) and an obelisk. The obelisk was erected in 1824 to mark the Greenwich meridian – the direction of true north from the telescope of the Royal Observatory at Greenwich. In 1850 the meridian changed, and 0 degrees longitude now passes nearer to the position of the trig point. But there is also a plaque attached to the obelisk, to commemorate T. E. Lawrence of Lawrence of Arabia fame.

Now we set off through the Hawk Wood

Lawrence of Arabia

T. E. Lawrence had a long and improbable association with Pole Hill. This peripatetic man has also attracted other monuments around the UK in unlikely spots from Dorset to Bridlington, but *Lawrence of Chingford* doesn't have quite the same numinous ring as David Lean's wide-screen epic of the desert. Lawrence owned 18 acres of land here, and had planned to build a house and printing press here, but the plan never came to fruition. But he did let his friend Vyvyan Richards build a wooden hut here on the top of Pole Hill called Cloisters, a substantial L-shaped dwelling with a garden and even a plunge pool, where he lived until 1922; the historic shack actually survives as a repository for forestry equipment at the Conservator's Yard in Loughton. In 1930, five years before his death, Lawrence sold Pole Hill to the Conservators of Epping Forest.

Cloisters on Pole Hill.

Chingford and the Sewardstone Hills 31

The summit of Pole Hill.

for the second, slightly hidden summit at Yardley Hill. With your back to the Obelisk, therefore, looking away from the view, take

The view from Pole Hill.

the path straight ahead into the woods and follow it to the left along a ridge and continue downhill past a dead tree that looks like a totem pole. Then take a right fork towards the edge of Chingford Golf Course which will appear ahead of you.

At the junction opposite a golf course green take the second path on your left downhill, and continue past a white sign on your right forbidding horse riding.

The path continues down to emerge onto open grassland. Cross the brook and follow the second path to the left towards a hilly meadow, passing yet another white sign forbidding horse riding. Head uphill across the meadow past a few clumpy overgrown trees on your left, and then take the path bearing to the right into the woods, and begin the short climb to the summit of Yardley Hill.

Continue until you reach a fork, and take the left-hand path along a ridge until you arrive in a grassy clearing at the peak. The view from Yardley Hill is well worth it:

The clearing at the summit of Yardley Hill.

spread out before you are splendid views of the two reservoirs and ahead, up on its hill in the distance, Alexandra Palace,

Crossing the meadow towards Yardley Hill.

which you can visit in the walk beginning on p. 13. To the left you can see the City, and beyond it the hills of south-east London, the Crystal Palace TV mast and the Croydon transmitter.

On to the third summit, which is a fair walk away. Retrace your steps back into the woodland until you reach the fork in the path. This time continue to

The 'totem pole tree' in Hawk Wood.

The top of Yates Meadow.

Gilwell Park

Gilwell Park is said to be the site of yet another royal hunting lodge, reputedly built by Henry VIII for his son Edward. The current house, however, dates to the eighteenth century and, together with 52 acres of land, was donated to the Scouts in 1919 after a scout commissioner had approached Robert Baden-Powell, the Scout Association's august founder, to point out that Scouts in the East End of London had no outdoor venue for their activities. When he was ennobled Baden-Powell took the name of Baron Baden-Powell of Gilwell Park. The complex remains a flagship outdoor and conference centre for the Scout Association.

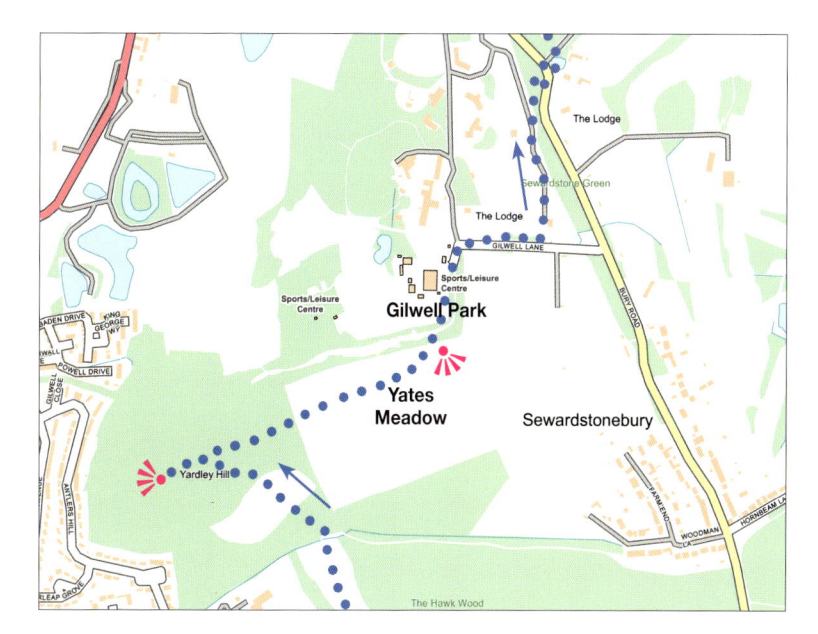

your left along the ridge, until you arrive at a crossroads of paths marked with a wooden post. Go straight across, through a gap in the hedge and out onto the verdant hillside of Yates Meadow. Head across the crest of the hill, and at the highest point of the meadow a solid bench offers the prime location to enjoy the views of the Hawk Wood, Epping Forest and, to the right, an extensive panorama of the London skyline.

Continue along the top of the meadow, and at the corner you have a choice: the path to the left towards Barn Hill, or you can stick at two summits and turn right to walk downhill to return to Chingford (see *, p. 38, below).

If you take the Barn Hill route, you will come out onto Gilwell Lane, at the perimeter of the Scout Association's permanent campsite and training centre at Gilwell Park.

Walk down Gilwell Lane past the HQ buildings and main entrance towards Bury Road. Just before you reach the road junction you will see a bridleway/path to the left through woodland, which you'll shortly find runs parallel to the road. At the end, you'll need to cross the road, aiming for the 'No Through Road' Green Lane directly opposite. Cross this road very carefully, and continue down the lane.

About 100 metres along the lane to your left you will see two logs blocking a path. Sidestep the logs and follow it through the sparse woodland to cross an unmade road to a field. This area is being developed as Sewardstone Park

Chingford and the Sewardstone Hills 35

Cemetery, so be careful of vehicles on the road. The path continues across the field uphill towards woods and the summit of Barn Hill. To your left are more spectacular views of the reservoirs. At the top a walk through the woods brings you out onto a grassland ridge – the unassertive summit of Barn Hill – and views out over Hertfordshire, Essex and Waltham Abbey. The distant hum of the M25 is ever-present. To your right beyond the tree-fringed edge of the cemetery rises Lippitt Hill, the final eminence of the Sewardstone Hills.

Continue along the grassy ridge path until it bears left downhill beside a patch of scrub towards the reservoirs, and out onto a gravel track. As the track enters open parkland turn left and follow the line

King George's Reservoir from Barn Hill.

The Lee Valley reservoirs.

of hedge across the hill and towards what is the cemetery road and a distant pond (Do not be tempted to follow the track downhill towards the main road in the near distance).

At the cemetery road turn left and follow uphill towards the car park for the

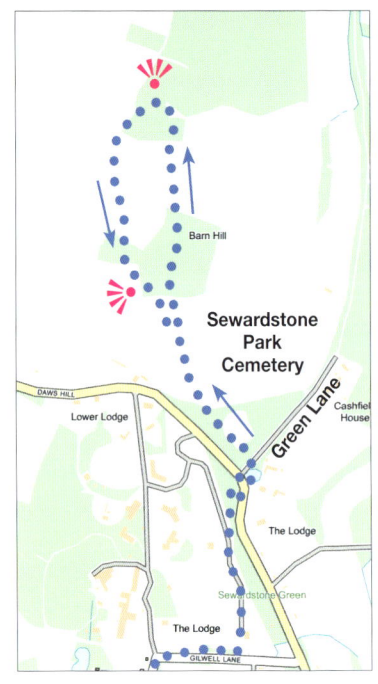

36 Reservoir Jogs

Garden of Firdaus Muslim cemetery. Head up towards the line of trees, and at the end of the car park follow the path to the left heading back up towards Barn Hill. Turn right over a stile marked London Loop into the trees, and then over yet another stile along a wire fence with extensive views of the reservoirs below. Over a third stile, and follow the path to the right and up some steps made of old railway sleepers. Now cross the cinder track and you are back out onto the familiar grassy slope. Retrace your steps across the field and back to Gilwell Lane and the Scout camp.

Beyond the scout camp turn left through 98 Gate Gilwell Lane to take you back towards Yates' Meadow.

The Garden of Firdaus.

Sewardstone Park Cemetery

This recently opened cemetery, on what was previously farmland, reflects a growing preference in society for a simpler, more natural resting place, whether for burial or the interment of ashes, where the existing landscape is given equal prominence with the siting of graves and memorials. The ideal is a parkland in harmony with the surrounding countryside, that will become a haven for wildlife and a place for quiet reflection and remembrance.

To minimise environmental impact, all memorials and grave markers are to be made of wood and blend in with the surroundings – the planting of trees and erecting of wildlife boxes and wooden benches is encouraged. There is also a designated 5-acre meadow specifically for Muslim burials. The great Nunhead Cemetery you'll encounter on the New Cross Gate–Forest Hill walk offers an instructive comparison with how they went about things in the nineteenth century.

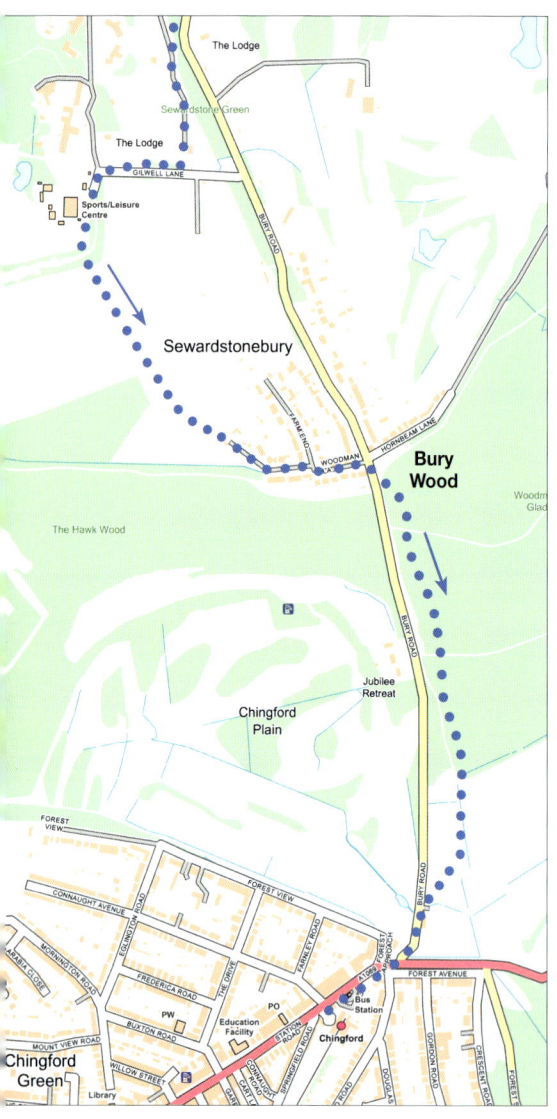

well-appointed houses sporting some equally high-end vehicles, and continue round to the junction with Bury Road. On the other side is Bury Wood and the great sweep of Epping Forest.

The last leg of our walk is entirely on the level – no more hill-climbing – and skirts the very edge of the forest.

Cross the road and take the forest path that follows Bury Road. Continue until you arrive at an expanse of grassy parkland. This is Chingford Plain, home to the Epping Forest Visitor Centre and Queen Elizabeth's Hunting Lodge – the first Queen Elizabeth, that is: Queen Bess was reportedly here too! In the summer months, in an ancient tradition revived in 2002, the plain is grazed by Longhorn cattle. If you are in need of refreshment there is a good café, the Larder at Butlers Retreat (open every day), next to the Hunting Lodge, which is the white building you can see up on the hill on the far side of the plain.

*Walk straight down the left-hand side of Yates' Meadow to the bottom. Go through the gate and follow the path uphill. At the top take the path to the left into Woodman Lane, past some large and very

Alternatively, walk across to the road – on the opposite side is Chingford Golf Course clubhouse. Cross the road and

The view north from the ridge along Barn Hill.

take the left-hand fork, Station Road, which leads you back to Chingford Station.

The descent of Yates Meadow from Gilwell Park.

Chingford and the Sewardstone Hills 39

The Wellingtonia Avenue, Havering Country Park.

❸

Five Parks Rising to a Peak

Romford to Havering Park

This walk is unique in this book as one of almost continuous ascent to reach its highest point, via a pleasant uphill walk through a string of municipal parks, formed from Havering's ancient private estates to realise an interwar local councillor's vision of a 'green lung' winding up through the borough. It is also, from within ten minutes of leaving Romford, almost entirely green and sylvan, culminating in a stretch of magnificent, landscaped parkland. The prospect south from Havering-atte-Bower, the village at the peak of the ridge, is superb, as are the subsequent views of the London skyline beyond Havering Country Park at the start of your descent. Other highlights are what must be one of the most stunning locations anywhere in the country for a village cricket ground, and a remarkable avenue of Giant Redwood trees.

Summits:
Orange Tree Hill, 105m – 17th highest point in London

Length: 5.4 miles – 9 km
Time: 3 hours
Total ascent: 396 feet – 120 metres
Start and finish: Romford Station – Elizabeth Line and British Rail. (The return is via a short bus ride from Havering Park).
Base camp: Numerous cafés close to Romford Station. Raphael Park has a restaurant/café and a coffee kiosk and public toilets. Bedfords Park has light refreshments in its visitor centre. The Orange Tree pub on Orange Tree Hill is a popular place and can be busy at weekends. Along the way there are numerous picnic spots.

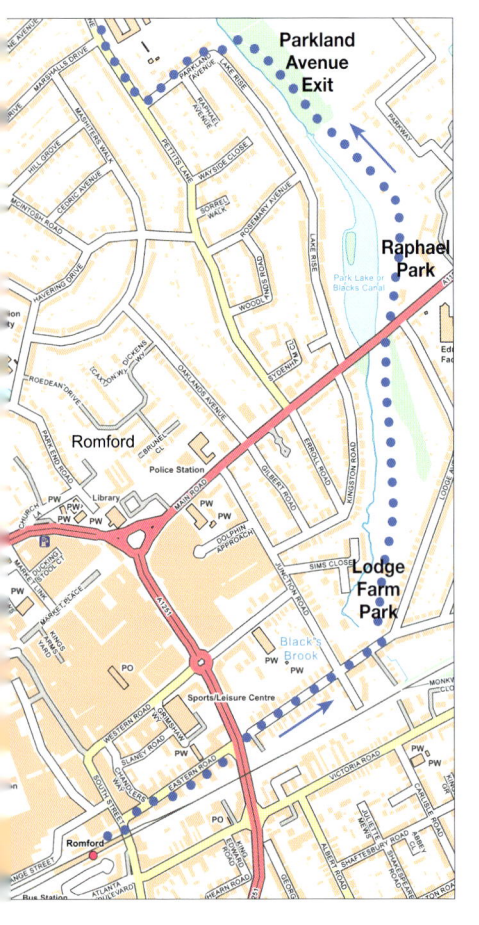

Once the Elizabeth Line has swished you to Romford in spacious, air-conditioned comfort, turn left out of the station and immediately right into Eastern Road. Cross the dual carriageway at the pedestrian crossing, on the other side of which Eastern Road continues. When you reach a junction carry straight on along Carlton Road. A hundred metres or so on the left-hand side of the road you'll find the car park and entrance to Lodge Farm Park. With the brief exception of crossing the busy A12, we'll now leave the urban environment behind for the remainder of our walk.

Take the path into the park, past a bowling green and the Havering Miniature Railway Club, whose miniature-gauge but surprisingly extensive track forms a 2.5km loop and is open to the public for rides two Sundays a month from Easter to October (rideonrailways.co.uk/hmrc). Soon there's a fork in the path: you can take either option, as both lead to the far end of the park. The exit from the park finds you on Main Road: cross it and you are immediately

42 Five Parks Rising to a Peak

at the entrance to Raphael Park.

The main path takes you alongside the lake past the bandstand and into a woodland walk, where you will immediately spy a quirky statue commemorating Percy the Park Keeper. The protagonist of the hugely popular picture books by Nick Butterworth – a local lad – and an animated TV series was supposedly inspired by an actual park keeper here at Raphael Park.

When you reach a signpost, you can

Raphael Park

The land that went to form Raphael Park, including the lake, was formerly part of Gidea Hall, a long-lost estate dating back to medieval times. The park was opened in 1904 and named after Sir Herbert Raphael, a local Liberal politician and property developer who donated the land.

Today this lovely, well-appointed landscape boasts a Green Flag award, signifying it has reached an internationally recognised standard for parks and green spaces, its classic features including the idyllic lake, an open-air theatre and a bandstand. Near the entrance, Raphael's Restaurant has a seriously foodie menu available all day, while there is a coffee kiosk and public toilets at the far end of the park.

either turn left to continue the walk by leaving the park at Parkland Avenue or, if you want to stop for basic refreshments, turn right and head uphill across the open grass. After your pit stop you'll need to retrace your steps back to the Parkland Avenue exit.

From Parkland Avenue turn right down Pettits Lane and head towards the junction with the A12 (you can already hear the roar of traffic). Cross this thunderous dual carriageway by the pedestrian bridge and turn right at the bottom by the shops. Turn left past the shops and look for the fire station on the other side of the road. Just past the fire station turn right into Beauly Way. Continue along the road until you see the entrance to Rise Park on the left-hand side of road. Turn left inside the

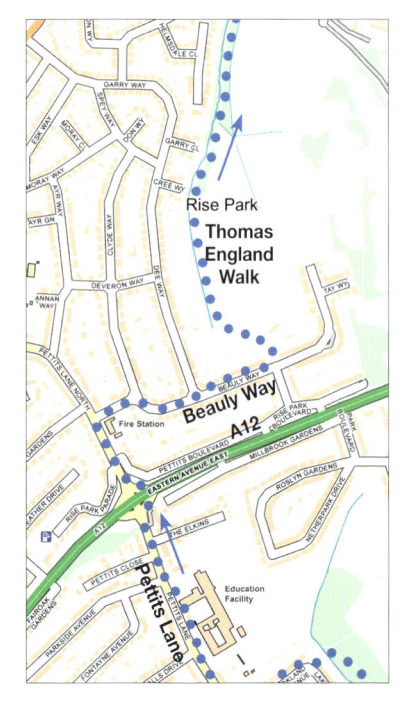

The London skyline from Bedford Park gate.

park to follow the waymarked 'Thomas England Walk'.

Rise Park was donated to the local community in 1937 by the local councillor and businessman Thomas England, who had a vision of a 'green lung' of connected parks running through the borough from Lodge Farm Park through to Bedfords Park. The commemoration walk itself was developed in the 1960s. Follow the woodland walk until you reach the road. Cross Lower Bedford Road at the lights and now enter Bedfords Park. This is where you really begin to climb.

On entering the park take the path uphill ahead of you, to climb a lush, hilly

Foxes Hill.

Bedfords Park

This superb and historic parkland of 215 acres was once part of the royal hunting grounds of Havering Palace, and yet another forgotten manorial estate that made way for a public park in the 1930s. Now designated a local nature reserve owing to its diverse landscapes – woodlands, marshes, meadows, and formal parkland – It is also home to a herd of red deer.

At the top end of the park, the visitor centre is run by Essex Wildlife Trust, and amenities include a café, shop and toilets – the terrace has great views over London. Close by is also an award-winning walled garden, one of the last vestiges of the old manor, lovingly tended by a dedicated team of volunteers.

Near the visitor centre.

Romford to Havering Park 45

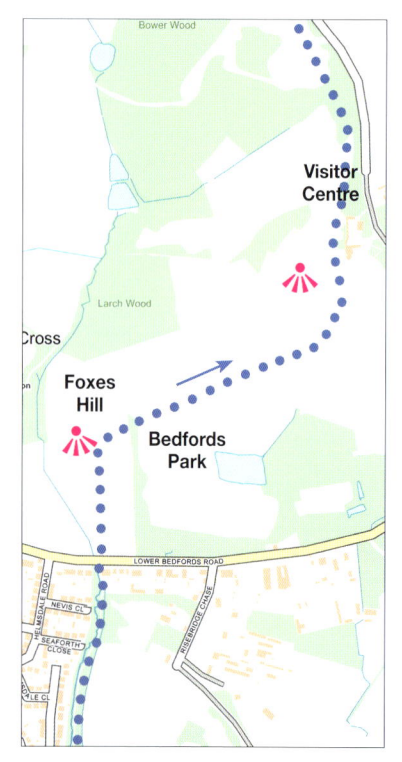

Elizabeth Bridge rising over the river at Dartford and beyond that the North Downs in Kent.

Take the path to the right downhill through a gate and continue straight ahead along the fence. Through the gate on the left you come out into a small copse, and then another gate takes you out into a meadow. Head across it to a gate on your right at the edge of the woods, but remember to turn round as you approach it for more fabulous views of the City, the Shard, the glittering towers of Canary Wharf and Docklands and, to the east, Shooters Hill. You might even catch a plane landing at or taking off from London City Airport.

Go through the gate and climb the steps uphill past the 'No. 6' signpost. At the junction of paths turn left uphill and out into open parkland.

Follow the path alongside the woods and eventually you'll see a car park to your right. The visitor centre is through the car park, and open 7 days a week from 10 a.m. to 5.00 p.m.

Past the car park follow the path ahead into woods, which is waymarked with an orange arrow and the number 12. Turn right, back into parkland, to find yourself walking along a pleasant swathe of greensward parallel to the road on your right. The benches along here provide a suitable picnic spot with sweeping parkland views. Ahead of you you'll see Havering Water Tower pointing above the

meadow known as Foxes Hill. Bower House, a Grade 1 Palladian villa on Orange Tree Hill, becomes visible in the distance. From the top of the hill views extend beyond the Thames, out of sight down in the valley, all the way to Shooters Hill and Woolwich in the south. To the east you can see the delicate tracery of the Queen

The Dartford Bridge from Foxes Hill.

Havering-atte-Bower's cricket ground on top of the world.

trees like a rocket.

Leave the park at the white gate and turn left along the path to the pavement alongside the road. You'll get a clear view now of the dramatic white water tower, built in 1931 and designed to look like a Norman tower. Owned by Essex and Suffolk Water, it is still in use and not open to the public.

It's worth a quick diversion into the Havering-atte-Bower cricket ground immediately to your left, which must be one of the most scenic cricket grounds in London, if not the whole country, the landscape dropping away beyond its far boundary with panoramic views out over London and the whole Thames river valley. No sightscreen at that end to block the view – but how would the umpire at the road end be able to concentrate on checking for no-balls and LBWs, and how many would Ben Stokes get for tonking the ball clean out of the ground high over mid-off and down the hillside for ever?

Back on the pavement you'll soon see Havering-atte-Bower's village green on the opposite side of road. You've now reached the top of Orange Tree Hill, one of the highest hills in London, and the crest of our walk.

On the green you will see signposts to the left to Orange Tree Hill, the road. If you want

The water tower.

Romford to Havering Park 47

refreshments at this point, down the road on the left you'll find the Orange Tree pub, a welcoming and very popular destination for food and drink, with a large outside seating area. At weekends tables might be hard to come by without booking.

Although it feels as though we're very much out in rural England by now and far from the metropolis, remarkably Havering-atte-Bower turns out to be served by red London buses – after a fashion. If you want to end your walk here at its highest point you can catch the little 375 up in the village or outside the pub to take you back to Romford – but check the timetable in advance: the frequency of a bus every hour and a half wouldn't go down well any further into the capital.

The London skyline on the horizon above Havering Park.

48   Five Parks Rising to a Peak

Looking towards central London from outside the village.

Havering-atte-Bower

The village green and the church stand on the site of Havering Palace. Built by Edward the Confessor, one of the last Saxon Kings in the eleventh century, it remained a royal palace until the English Civil War, when the land was divided and sold, and the palace eventually demolished. St John's the Evangelist Church dates from 1874, but does boast a Norman bowl in its font, a relic from the chapel of Havering Palace. The olde-worlde stocks and whipping post situated in the south-east corner of the village green are of course reproductions, and only appeared in 1966.

In 1828 the McIntosh family purchased the land from the Crown and developed it with an Italianate mansion and formal parkland, the centrepiece of which was the planting of the Wellingtonia Avenue, which we'll soon come to on this walk: a spectacular natural archway of Giant Redwood trees (Wellingtonia being part of the species' original name, in erroneous homage to the Duke of Wellington).

Although the mansion was demolished in 1925 and the family's fortune and influence disappeared, over a hundred of the trees remain, forming the second largest plantation in England of one of the tallest species in the world. Nowadays the avenue sits at the centre of Havering Country Park.

The London skyline as you emerge from Havering Country Park.

Back on the village green the walk continues through the churchyard. Go out through the back gate, turn right and then left onto a wide lane heading downwards, with great views of the rolling Essex countryside to your right, and you'll enter Havering Country Park. Head straight on and you will find yourself in the amazing natural cathedral of Wellingtonia Avenue – over a hundred Wellingtonias or Giant Redwoods, many over a hundred in age, their foliage closing high above your head in a bosky vaulting. When you meet Park Cross Road head along a path signposted 'Mud Hill' and head downhill.

You come out of the wood to splendid views spreading out right across London, all the way over to Forest Hill and Crystal Palace and the Croydon transmitter masts in the South. There's also a rare view of the Millennium Dome nestled in the river valley. Immediately across the valley to the west is Hainault Forest Country Park.

Turn left and head down the lane that tracks the edge of the wood. This eventually continues into a tarmac road that takes you past light industrial works and into a housing estate. This is Havering Park. At the crossroads you come to on Clockhouse Lane there is a choice of buses back to Romford Station: at the stop on the left you can catch the 365, while in Firbank Road on your right there's the 294.

50   Five Parks Rising to a Peak

A Wellingtonia or Giant Redwood in Havering Country Park.

London's 20 Highest Hills

This table omits other summits in the immediate vicinity - e.g. Kenwood House, as very near Hampstead Heath, Spaniards Road.

No.	Name	Borough	Height (metres)
1	South Street	Bromley	220
2	Sanderstead Plantation	Croydon	175
3	Littleheath Woods	Croydon	160
4	Stanmore	Harrow	152
5	Arkley	Barnet	147
6=	Highwood Hill, Totteridge Fields	Barnet	145
=	Harrow Weald Common	Harrow	145
7	Addington Hills	Croydon	142
8	Big Wood, Little Woodcote	Sutton	139
9	Hampstead Heath, West of Spaniards Road	Camden	137
10	Highgate, North Hill	Haringey	136
11	Shooters Hill	Greenwich	132
12=	Pinner Hill	Harrow/Hillingdon	125
=	Scratchwood	Barnet	125
13	Harrow-on-the-Hill	Harrow	124
14	Bournwell Hill	Barnet/Enfield	115
15	Sydenham Hill (Crystal Palace)	Lewisham/Southwark	112
16	Forest Hill	Lewisham	106
17=	Orange Tree Hill	Havering	105
=	Muswell Hill	Haringey	105

Whitechapel Mount

⑪

A lost hill of London, remembered only in a street name

Next to the original Royal London Hospital buildings on Whitechapel Road, Mount Terrace E1 is its only legacy. But what was it?

By the eighteenth century the Mount had become a prominent London landmark and tourist attraction, commanding views over Limehouse and Shadwell. But why it was there is open to debate. Its presence was first documented in the seventeenth century, and there are theories that it was the site of a Civil War fort, onto which debris from the rebuilding of London after the Great Fire was deposited.

The Mount was demolished in 1801 when the land was needed to accommodate the expanding city. Eventually the London Hospital spread onto the site, and archaeological work has since uncovered no new evidence to reveal its origins.

WHITECHAPEL MOUNT, FROM A DRAWING MADE IN 1801.

The Hills of the City of London ⑫

Summits: Ludgate Hill 17.6m; Cornhill 17.7m; Tower Hill 14.5m

The three ancient hills of the City – Ludgate Hill, Cornhill and Tower Hill – were the site of Roman London, and are now the names of districts and streets in the modern City of London. The walk between them is quite gentle, and you'd be hard pressed to pick out the contours of individual hills. Cornhill in fact has the highest peak at 17.7 metres, St Paul's Cathedral is built on the top of Ludgate Hill and Tower Hill is the site of Tower of London.

From this central ridge little streets run down to the river, and many of these are picturesquely named hills: Snow Hill, Dowg Hill, Garlick Hill, Lambeth Hill, White Lion Hill, Fish Street Hill, St Mary le Hill.

Garlick Hill.

Roman London

In Roman times London stretched from what is now Ludgate Circus only as far as Aldgate, restricting itself to the defensible vantage-point of the City's three hills. Several remarkable relics of Roman London can be visited today: the Mithraeum – the temple of Mithras, god of light – in Walbrook, beneath the Bloomberg building, the Roman amphitheatre underneath the Guildhall, and a section of the Roman city wall outside Tower Hill Tube.

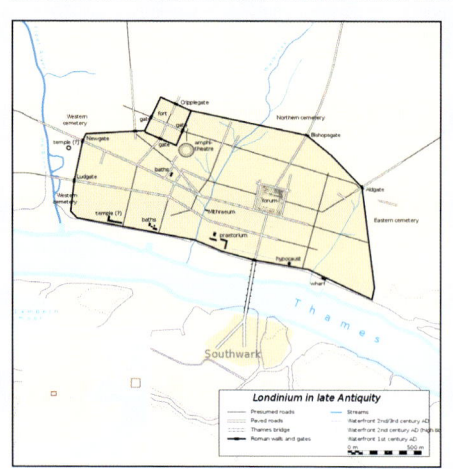

54 The Hills of the City of London

Bridge Street leading up onto Tower Hill.

St Paul's Cathedral at the top of Ludgate Hill.

Beckton Alps

⑬

Summit: 35m

It was an odd sight, as you sped eastwards along the A13, to see people skiing. But from 1989 a dry ski slope was indeed the incarnation of this artificial hill in East London, the highest in the capital. Those with longer memories will remember it – indeed, a much more extensive mound – as a toxic spoil heap for the huge Beckton Gas Works.

The ski centre shut in 2011, but the scuzzy summit used to be a striking vantage point for watching planes take off and land at nearby London City Airport,

The old ski slope, with London City Airport on the horizon to the right.

and for a London skyline with, oddly, the Shard well to the right of Canary

Beckton Gas Works

In 1949 this was the largest gas works in the world, stretching over 550 acres, and consuming a million tons of coal a year, brought down by sea from the Durham coalfield, the site chosen for its proximity to Barking Creek, where the coasters could dock. Part of the extensive railway system serving the works has been repurposed as the Beckton branch of the DLR.

After closure in 1976 the works' post-industrial dereliction saw it become a numinous film-set, staging John Wayne car chases in *Brannigan*, the opening sequence in the Bond film *For Your Eyes Only*, and transformed into a Viet Cong town for Stanley Kubrick's *Full Metal Jacket*.

The full extent of the old spoil heap.

Wharf. Since a noughties plan for a hotel development failed to materialise the Alps have been securely fenced off, and once again are best seen from the A13.

Beckton Alps 57

Stave Hill

Summit: 9m
Start and finish: Surrey Quays Station – Overground

The extensive network of the Surrey Docks finally closed in 1969. Most of the docks – several of them, like Canada Dock and Norway Dock, named after the provenance of most of the cargoes they handled – were filled in during the 1980s and became the Surrey Quays housing development, but imaginative uses have been found for others. Greenland Dock remains a strikingly large stretch of water, and is now home to a watersports centre, while the old Russia Dock, between Rotherhithe and Surrey Quays, has been re-landscaped as woodland and wildlife haven.

The centrepiece is Stave Hill, an artificial mound created from reclaimed waste and rubble. A relief map centred on the top of the hill gives a detailed relief map of the old docks and their exotic and dubious origins: in the eighteenth century Greenland Dock was a base for north Arctic whalers; along with the Baltic and Russia Docks it gave way to the nineteenth-century trade in timber.

It may only be 9 metres in altitude, but from its viewing platform Stave Hill offers a stunning 360-degree panorama of the London skyline. Here is probably the most arresting prospect to be had of Canary Wharf, and to the west the landmarks of the City, from St Paul's Cathedral to the Gherkin, are arrayed before you, all the way to the Strata Building at Elephant and Castle, and St Olave's church, Rotherhithe to the east. There is a rare side-on view of

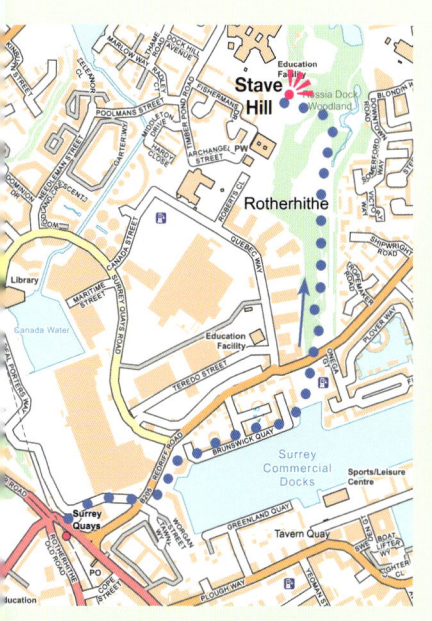

Tower Bridge and, peeking through the Rotherhithe gasometer, an equally rare view of the Monument next to the BT Tower. Back from the river you can see the churches of East London: St Paul's, Shadwell, St Mary's, Cable Street and St Anne's, Limehouse.

Stave Hill is most easily reached by a 10-minute walk from Surrey Quays Overground station via Greenland Dock and the Russia Dock woods. Rather than re-tracing your steps, you can walk to Rotherhithe Overground Station via the Thames Path.

The Royal Observatory, from the foot of Greenwich Park.

4

Three Rivers and Four Hills (including Octavia)

Brockley to Greenwich

This walk is one of two following the great ridge that sweeps across south-east London, and finishes above, and with the best views anywhere in this book of, the mighty River Thames. The neighbourhoods along the way range from the leafy gentility of Hilly Fields to the powerhouse high-density high-rise shooting up in the centre of Lewisham, and the green space from the local intimacy of Hilly Fields to the internationally renowned landmark of Greenwich Park. But it is the London rivers you come upon – three in all – that are perhaps most instructive, showing you, as you look down or descend from on high, why low ground is low: because it has a river running through it.

Summits:
Hilly Fields, 53m
Blackheath, 40m
Greenwich Park, 45m

Length: 4.5 miles – 7 kilometres
Time: 2½ hours
Total ascent: 302 feet – 92 metres
Start: Brockley Station – British Rail and Overground
Finish: Greenwich Station – British Rail and DLR
Base camp: Cafés at Brockley Station, Hilly Fields, Lewisham, Blackheath village and Greenwich Park, including the Royal Observatory.

Exit Brockley Station on the east (southbound) side into pedestrianised Coulgate Street – immediately in front of you are a couple of good local coffee shops, Broca and Browns, and a bar/bistro. In recent years this station frontage has been transformed by pedestrianisation and landscaping, and completed by the five Persian silk trees planted around the piazza by the Lewisham community-based charity, Street Trees for Living, who through public sponsorship have overseen the planting of 2,000 new trees throughout the borough. In summer they burst into fabulous deep-pink flower.

Leave Coulgate Street at the right-hand end of the street, past the Bob

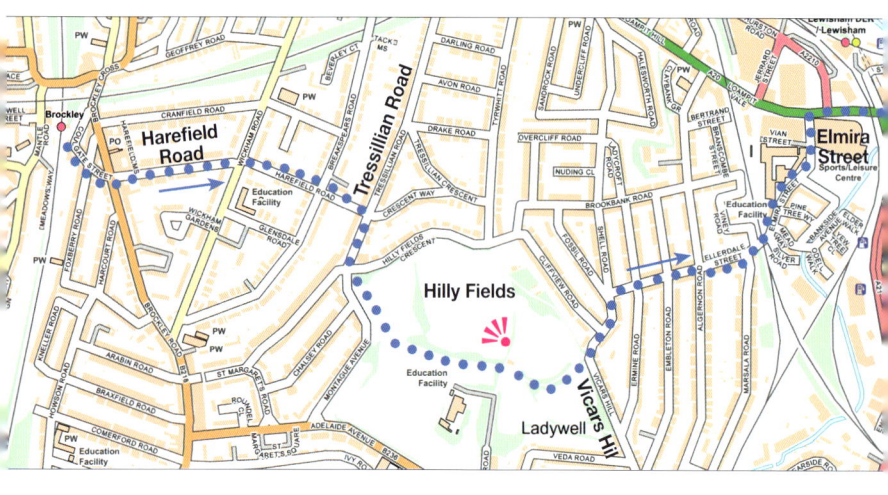

The pink Persian silk trees at Brockley Station.

62 Three Rivers and Four Hills (including Octavia)

Marley mural on your left, painted by Dale Grimshaw. The mural sits on the back wall of the local Wetherspoon's, the Brockley Barge, so-called because Brockley Station, and indeed the railway cutting in which it sits, was once on the site of the short-lived 9-mile-long Croydon Canal that opened in 1809 and ran from Croydon to the Grand Surrey Canal near Deptford Dock. It closed just 27 years later, and the land was sold to the London and Croydon Railway.

Cross Brockley Road and proceed uphill up Harefield Road next to Brockley Royal Mail Sorting Office, which takes you into the leafy neighbourhood of Hilly Fields. Continue over Wickham Road (once home to Kate Bush) and Breakspears Road, then at the junction turn right along Tressillian Road. On the north side of this road you'll pass another of Street Trees for Living's many local plantings: in this case a rare (at least on a street) foxglove tree, which blooms with unforgettable blue flowers. At the summit of the road, you find yourself facing the entrance to Hilly Fields.

Hilly Fields and Octavia Hill

In the late nineteenth century, the vast suburban expansion that followed the arrival of the railway in Brockley meant the farm on this hillside site was in danger of being swallowed up. Divine intervention came in the shape of Octavia Hill, the English social reformer and co-founder of the National Trust.

Hill had campaigned against building on woodlands and open spaces – Hampstead Heath and Parliament Hill were also saved in part due to her efforts (see p. 149). In the case of Hilly Fields, she was instrumental in raising subscriptions from the great and the good, including William Morris, that would eventually lead to the purchase of the land and secure its future as a public space. The park was eventually opened in 1896, following a major redesign by Lt Colonel J. J. Sexby, the doyen of late Victorian park design.

In 2020, to celebrate 125 years since the founding of the National Trust, walnut trees were planted on the lower flank of Hilly Fields.

The Crystal Palace ridge from the top of Hilly Fields.

Follow the path uphill and across the top ridge. From here the views stretch to Forest Hill, One Tree Hill, the Crystal Palace and Croydon transmitters and Beckenham on the south side, and, to the north, poking through the trees, the soaring expanse of the City, Canary Wharf, Docklands and the Millennium Dome. Also to the west the hill

The 'henge' at Hilly Fields.

High-rise Lewisham from the eastern edge of Hilly Fields.

of Nunhead Cemetery (visited on p. 81) is visible.

It is here on Hilly Fields that you can fully appreciate the expanse of the ridge that forms this part of south-east London's topography, stretching from Shooters Hill across to Greenwich and Blackheath, punctured by the River Ravensbourne valley at Lewisham and then rising again to form Hilly Fields, Telegraph Hill, Nunhead, Honor Oak, Forest Hill and Denmark Hill. You can walk more of it in the New Cross-Forest Hill walk.

The path brings you to a café nestled under the trees, an excellent place to stop and renowned for its cakes. To the right of the path you'll notice an intriguing 'henge' of stones arranged in the grass in a circle. It is in fact a granite stone sundial, erected to mark the millennium, which has since become a focal point for local celebrations. The 12 boulders were transported from Mount Struie near Scotsburn in Scotland. A little further to the south is a trig point, now fetchingly decorated with painted flowers.

Continue straight on along the path, now following the curve of the hill downwards. Ahead of you is the concrete jungle of Lewisham's new tower blocks, which has shot up in recent years and is becoming ever denser, and beyond that the distant Shooters Hill.

Leave the park through the gate to come out at the top of a long snaking road named Vicars Hill. Don't turn right, but continue straight on past Fossil Road and Shell Road on your left until the road becomes Ellerdale Street. Under the railway arch past the Ladywell sign you'll find yourself in Elmira Street on the edge of Lewisham. Follow it round onto Loampit Vale and turn right – don't worry: you won't be on this clogged stretch of the A20 for long. Cross the road at the crossing just before the railway bridge.

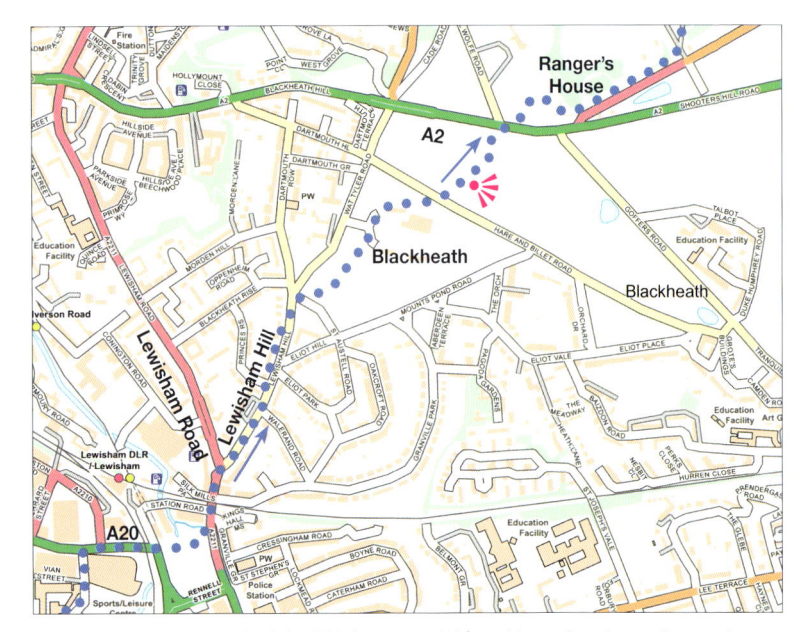

Head towards Lewisham Station (where you can truncate the walk if you wish) and, just after the station road, take a path to the left that leads along a river. It is here, at this unprepossesing spot hemmed in by railway viaducts and new-build high-rises, that you're at the confluence of two rivers. Coming in from the left is the River Ravensbourne (which rises in Keston near Bromley); from the right is the River Quaggy (which rises at Locksbottom near Orpington). They join here before heading to the River Thames at Deptford. This is the lowest point of our walk.

At the end of the path turn left into Lewisham Road and right at the roundabout into Lewisham Hill. You're now starting the climb up our second hill, towards Blackheath.

At the junction of St Austell Road the

The confluence of the Ravensbourne and the Quaggy near the foot of Lewisham Hill.

66 Three Rivers and Four Hills (including Octavia)

Blackheath

It's a popular urban myth that Blackheath is the site of mass plague burial pits, but there is no historic evidence to support this. The name is probably a corruption of the Old English words for 'black soil' or 'bleak heath' – not surprising given the high density of gravel hereabouts.

The heath has been a significant place of assembly and dissent through the ages. In 1381 during the Peasants' Revolt Wat Tyler's 100,000 anti-poll tax rebels gathered here before marching on London, where they were defeated. More shockingly, in 1497 it was the site of the Battle of Blackheath, where over 2,000 were killed when a rebellion of Cornishmen angry at being taxed for the Scottish wars was suppressed.

Subsequently, Blackheath was a mustering point for British armies heading overseas and the favoured place for royalty to be received: Henry V welcomed back here after Agincourt, and Charles II meeting the citizens of London after the Restoration.

Most famously nowadays, in April the heath is the start for the 40,000 runners in the London Marathon.

Noteworthy Georgian buildings dotted around the heath include the Grade II-listed Pagoda in Pagoda Gardens, built in 1770 and the home of Caroline of Brunswick when she separated from the Prince Regent in 1799, before she moved to the now-demolished Montague House, next to the Ranger's House. On the east-side of the heath is the Grade I-listed Paragon, a Bath-like crescent built in 1800.

expanse of the Blackheath plateau begins to appear. This was the site of the Eliot pit, one of two large gravel extraction pits, the other being the Vanbrugh pit on the north-east side that scarred the heath during the eighteenth century. This activity was halted in 1866 by the Metropolitan Commons Act, enacted to protect common land around London.

Cross onto the heath – the uneven contours are the vestiges of the excavations – skirting the Army Cadet Training centre on your right, to behold the full stretch of the heath. To your right, Blackheath village and All Saints' Church nestle against the backdrop

Greenwich Park. Blackheath Village teems with coffee shops, pubs and restaurants, if you want to stop for a break, and the railway station can link you back with central London.

Now we head for Greenwich. Cross the A2, or Shooters Hill Road as it's called round here. This ancient London artery, named Watling Street by the Romans, divides the heath from Greenwich Park, and was a notorious spot for highwaymen including Dick Turpin, who terrorised travellers in the early eighteenth century.

Aim for the Ranger's House, a smart Georgian villa now in the care of English Heritage and custodian to the treasure

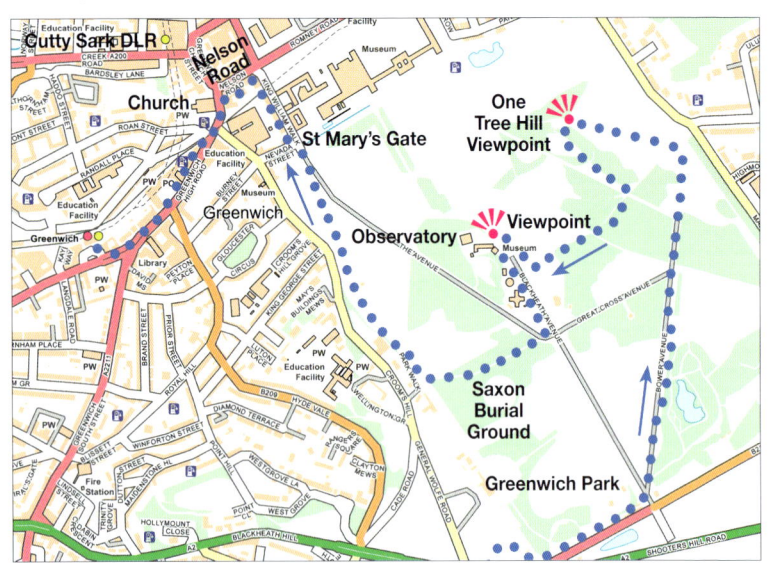

of the new Kidbrooke Village housing development and Shooters Hill. To the north is the Ranger's House, the busy A2 that regrettably transects the heath, and

trove that is the Wernher Collection, a fabulous and quirky collection of fine and decorative art, including porcelain, jewellery, furniture and tapestries,

Greenwich Park

One of London's oldest Royal parks, Greenwich Park has seen human settlement since Roman times, although recent archaeological work has been focused on the Saxon cemetery, which contains 31 burial mounds. During the reign of Henry V the park was used as royal hunting grounds, but it was Henry VI who established the Royal Palace at Greenwich by the river, on the site these days occupied by the Old Naval College, a campus of Greenwich University. The Royal Palace was the birthplace of Henry VIII and both his daughters, Elizabeth and Mary. During Henry VIII's residence the park was greatly developed for riding and hunting. Deer are still a feature of the park.

The original palace was knocked down after the English Civil War, but the royal connection continued during the reign of Charles II with the establishment in the park of the Royal Observatory, the Royal Hospital School (now the National Maritime Museum) and the Inigo Jones-designed Queen's House.

amassed by Julius Wernher in the nineteenth century. Once there, follow the wall and line of trees to your right and you will find Chesterfield Gate, one of many entrances to Greenwich Park, at the corner of Chesterfield Walk and Charlton Way.

From the gate take the path to the right through a lightly wooded area, beautiful with camellias in the spring, with a cricket field on your left. This brings you to Blackheath Avenue (just by the toilets) and the main park entrance. Cross the road and take the broad path on your left that skirts the flower garden and the pond. Now you are aiming toward the remains of the Roman Temple and Maze Hill Gate – there are plenty of signposts. Just before the gate you need to take the second path on your left, which climbs steeply up to One Tree Hill.

On the summit here you'll have your first view of the Thames – and it's spectacular. To the east you'll see the cross-river cable car, planes heading towards City Airport, the Dome, the Optic Cloak (a bold aluminium sculpture by Conrad Shawcross), the squat, four chimneyed Greenwich Power Station and the wide bend in the river round the Isle of Dogs.

Take the winding path downhill, and then turn left uphill again along a wooded avenue called Lovers' Walk. At the top is an Elizabeth I Oak (yes, another one in addition to One Tree Hill's at Honor Oak on p. 83). Turn right and follow the path towards Blackheath Avenue, and then right along that towards the Royal Observatory.

Moonrise over One Tree Hill.

The London skyline at sunset from the Observatory viewpoint.

The Royal Observatory

In 1675 Charles II commissioned Sir Christopher Wren to build the Royal Observatory at the top of Greenwich Park on the site of a medieval watchtower, the perfect vantage point for studying the heavens. John Flamsteed was appointed as the first Astronomer Royal, with the mission to map the night sky and find longitude: the east–west position of a point on the globe that would be invaluable for accurate nautical navigation.

The close relation of timekeeping and the mapping of stars led a century later to the development of the chronometer (a maritime clock), and the nautical tables which allowed navigators to chart their position anywhere on the globe. In 1884 there was worldwide adoption of Greenwich as the Prime Meridian (mean) or 0 degrees longitude, from where all time zones (Greenwich Mean Time) and degrees of longitude could be measured.

Now part of Royal Museums of Greenwich, the observatory boasts one of the largest telescopes in the world. Built in 1893, the 28-inch refractor was groundbreaking in its day. Here you can stand on the Meridian line and see the clocks and chronometers used to solve the longitude riddle.

Next to the Royal Observatory is the viewpoint, which has one of the most dramatic, must-see hilltop views in London. The swathe of parkland leading downhill to the National Maritime Museum, the Queen's House and the Naval College was landscaped in the seventeenth century by the same landscape architect, André Le Notre, who designed the gardens at Versailles. A large-scale restoration programme is in progress. In 2012 this was the striking location and backdrop of the equestrian events at the London Olympics.

The views out across to Canary Wharf and Docklands show the full sweep and snaking path of the river. To the left is the City, with the Gherkin, the Walkie-Talkie, 22 Bishopsgate, St Paul's Cathedral; further round is the Shard. Beyond are the hills of Hampstead, which you can visit on the walk on p. 147.

From the Observatory viewpoint you have a choice. The shorter option is to follow the path down the hill to the bottom of the park to leave it at St Mary's Gate for the centre of Greenwich.

Or you can explore further. Turn back

Canary Wharf beyond the Old Naval College.

into the main avenue and, at the end of the Observatory buildings, take a path downhill to your right and you will find yourself on the lower Avenue (more toilets). Take the path to left and you will be close to the Saxon burial ground. When you reach Croom's Hill Gate you can either turn right uphill to explore the Rose Garden, or left and continue downhill until you reach St Mary's Gate.

For transport options continue ahead along William Walk with the Maritime Museum on your right, then turn left at a branch of Gail's bakery into Nelson Road.

At the junction with Greenwich Church Street turn right if you want the DLR: you'll see Cutty Sark DLR on the opposite side of the road next to Waterstones. For the railway station turn left, into Greenwich High Road, and cross over near the church (St Alfege, the first church to be designed by Sir Nicholas Hawksmoor, and well worth a visit). At the fork in the road past the cinema keep right, and soon you'll see a Travelodge and Greenwich Station and DLR.

Nine Elms beyond the River Thames.

Shooters Hill

⑮

Summit: 132m – 11th highest in London
Start and finish: Woolwich or Woolwich Arsenal Stations (Elizabeth Line or British Rail/DLR) via 244 bus to the Shrewsbury Lane stop on Shooters Hill Road.

This distinctive hill in south-east London rises above Blackheath, and its landmark water tower is visible from many viewpoints in the east of the capital.

It features in established long-distance walks like the Capital Ring and the Green Chain Walk, and has many treasures worth exploring, but the downside is that there are no railway stations close, Woolwich and Falconwood being the nearest.

Along the hill's south flank runs the ancient woodland of Oxleas Wood, a Site of Special Scientific Interest as parts of it date back over 7,000 years. In the 1990s the wood was saved from virtual destruction for a cross-river road scheme by mass protests and civil action.

The rest of the hill and woodland are made up of the grounds and gardens of several demolished mansions, with the greatest prize being the newly refurbished folly, Severndroog Castle, which can be ascended to its rooftop viewing platform on Sundays afternoons, when its café is also open.

The Oxleas Wood Café is arrestingly situated at the top of the hill looking out on a sweeping meadow.

Views extend to the south-west towards Croydon, Crystal Palace and the ridge that forms Forest Hill and Hilly Fields. To the south and south-east can be seen the Surrey and Kent stretches of the North Downs.

The Oxleas Wood Café at the top of Shooters Hill.

Royal Arsenal West

244 Bus Route from Woolwich

Woolwich

Woolwich Arsenal

Shooters Hill Bus Stop

Severndroog Castle

Oxleas Wood

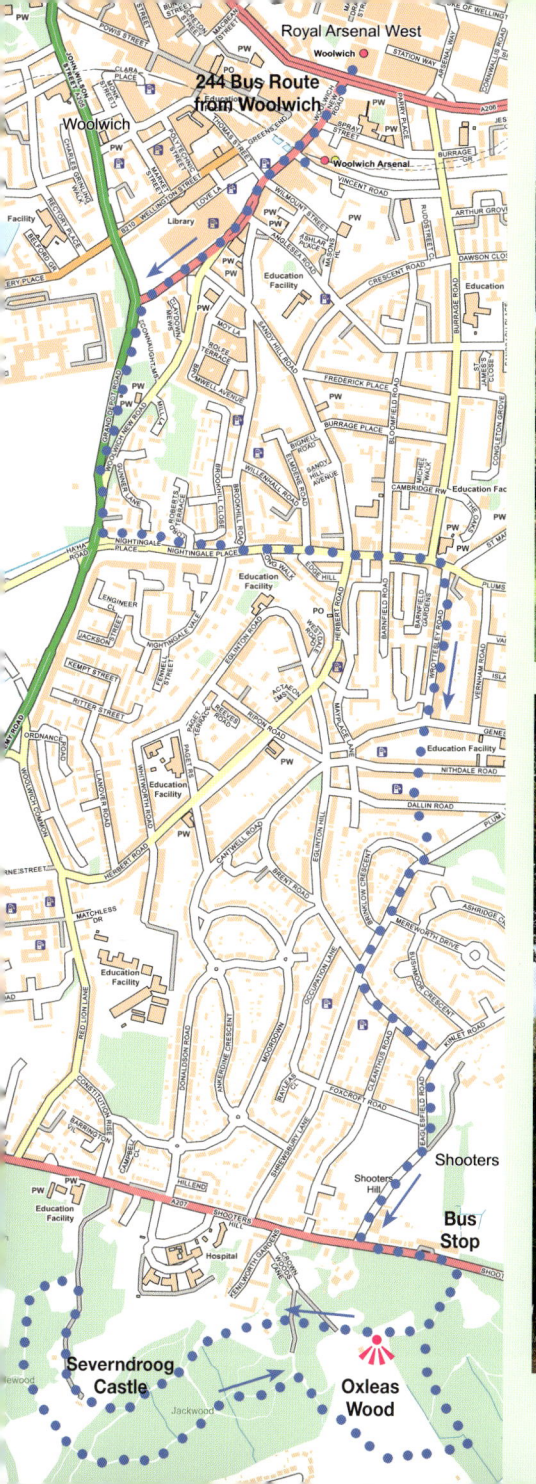

The gardens of Jack Wood House, one of the demolished mansions on Shooters Hill.

Severndroog Castle.

Shooters Hill 75

The towers of Canary Wharf looming above Jerningham Road, New Cross.

❺

Telegraphs, Beacons and Masts

New Cross Gate to Forest Hill

This is a walk of proper hills, both in place names and gradients: there are steep ascents and inclines from start to finish. It is the best way to walk some of the natural ridge that winds across south-east London all the way from Shooters Hill to Sydenham Hill in the south-west and out towards Denmark Hill in the west, formed of London Clay-covered chalk hills created around 50 million years ago. Parts of London are pretty flat; this is definitely, and primarily, *hilly*.

It's a landscape of handsome and prosperous Victorian and Edwardian houses, some fine (and hilly) parks and green spaces, and one that, more than any in this book, will bring home to you the human advantages of high ground. In more ancient times they built castles and fortresses on top of hills, for the best sight of the enemy; in Napoleonic times they built a string of telegraph stations on these hills in order to relay news from the battlefield and ship movements in the channel. These days we still site television masts and radio masts on the highest ground: you'll see those along and near this walk.

Summits:
Telegraph Hill, 50m
Nunhead Cemetery, 60m
One Tree Hill, 82m
Horniman Museum, 86m
Forest Hill, 106m – 16th highest point in London

Length: 4.5 miles – 7 kilometres
Time: 2½ hours
Total ascent: 440 feet – 134 metres
Start: New Cross Gate Station – British Rail and Overground
Finish: Forest Hill Station – British Rail and Overground
Base camp: Cafés all along the route.

Leave New Cross Gate Station, a buzzy hub thanks to the student population at nearby Goldsmiths College, part of the University of London, and cross the perennially traffic-clogged A2 at the pedestrian crossing outside. Turn right, then first left into the London plane-lined Jerningham Road for the ascent of Telegraph Hill. This walk sets you climbing, and steeply, straight away.

Not far up on your right, on the wall of Haberdasher's Hatcham College, is a plaque commemorating the poet Robert Browning, who once lived in a cottage at the foot of Telegraph Hill. Halfway up the hill, if the leaves are off the trees, you can admire Goldsmiths College's steel 'scribble', a 30-foot-tall sculpture perched

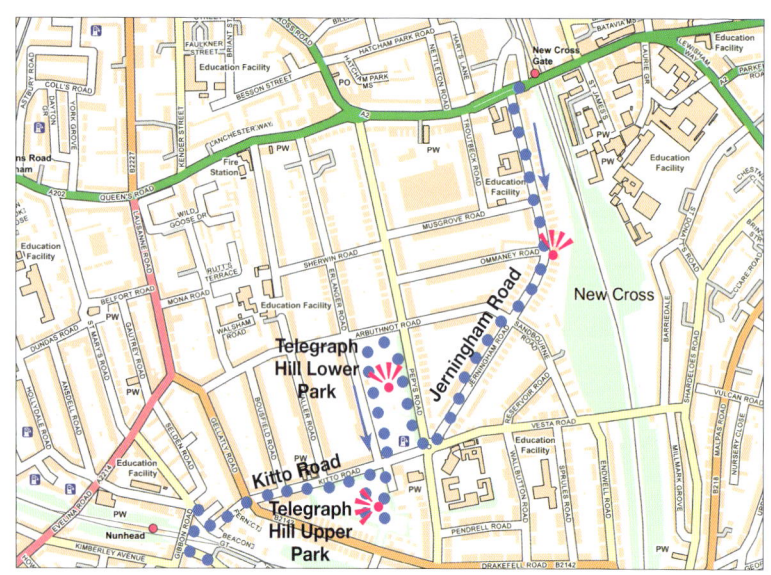

78 TELEGRAPHS, BEACONS AND MASTS

on the Art Department roof, designed by Will Alsop. The sculpture is composed of 229 separate pieces of metal, weighs 25 tonnes, has 72 twists and if unravelled would measure 534 metres, or twice the height of Canary Wharf's Canada Square Tower (which can also be seen). On this walk more than others the London's landmarks appear among the trees and the buildings

At the roundabout at the top of the hill you'll see to your left the entrance to Lower Telegraph Hill Park, from which you the Shard is visible. On Saturdays a Farmer's market is held here between 10 and 3. For a quick circuit of this pleasantly uphill-winding park start with the path downhill to your right past the basketball court and look-out point. Continue slightly uphill and you'll see the London Eye, Westminster Abbey, BT Tower and the Shard, all the way round to the Gherkin and the City, although tree cover may obscure this in the summer.

At the end of the park take the path downwards and left past the children's playground. At the pond cross the wooden bridge to the left and look out for a visiting heron. Turn left and head uphill to the gate ahead. Opposite and next to St Catherine's Church is the Hill Station café, a scenic place to stop if you're already in need of refreshment.

The entrance to Upper Telegraph Hill Park is just to the right of the Hill Station opposite the gate you've just exited. Take the path to your right below the tennis courts, and then a left across the park. It's worth scrambling up the escarpment onto the plateau above where the views are best. This time you have totally uninterrupted views to the west across to St George's Tower and the Nine Elms development as well as all the central London landmarks. If you look to the far west you can see on the most distant point of the ridge the Salvation Army's William Booth College at Denmark Hill, designed by Sir

Lower Telegraph Hill Park.

Upper Telegraph Hill Park.

New Cross Gate to Forest Hill 79

Telegraph Hill

Telegraph Hill gained its name from a naval semaphore telegraph station that was situated in what is now Upper Telegraph Park in 1795 at the height of the Napoleonic Wars. It was the third in the chain of stations that stretched from the Admiralty in Whitehall to Admiralty House at 36 West Square in Lambeth, and then to Telegraph Hill and on to Shooters Hill, Swanscombe and Gads Hill, then across Kent diverting to both Sheerness and Deal.

The system involved a chain of buildings in prominent positions with eight shutters on their roofs each 6 metres high, which were opened and closed in various combinations corresponding to letters or words. Its inventor, Lord George Murray, boasted that messages could be passed from one end to the other in 60 seconds. The high point was the signalling of Wellington's victory at Waterloo in 1815. With the advent of the railway network the system was finally retired in 1836.

Giles Gilbert Scott (also the architect of the Royal Star and Garter Home in Richmond – see p. 110 – and Battersea Power Station), opened in 1929.

Nowadays this park is a favoured spot for sunset picnics, but you can see why it was chosen for the telegraph station.

Head down Kitto Road, crossing over Drakefell Road by Skehans pub; Kitto Road continues on a dogleg to Gibbon Road and Nunhead Station (trains to central London or Kent). Opposite the station turn left into Oakdale Road, which climbs to a mini

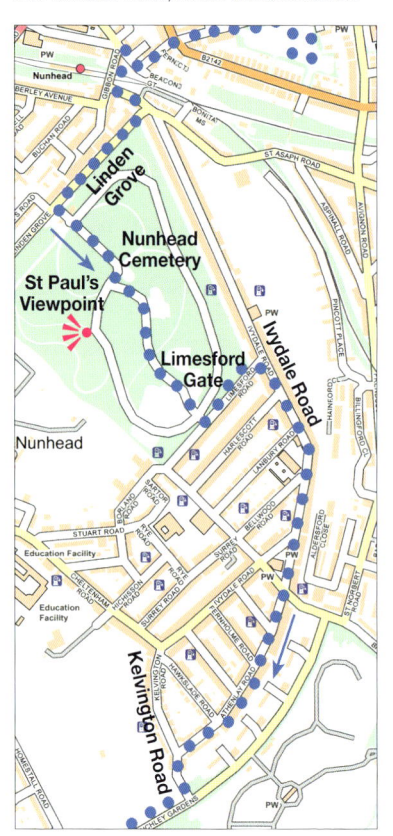

Nunhead Cemetery

Consecrated in 1840, Nunhead is known as one of the 'magnificent seven' Victorian cemeteries of London (the others being Kensal Green, Highgate, West Norwood, Abney Park, Brompton and Tower Hamlets), and at 52 acres is the second largest.

During the first half of the nineteenth century London's population had more than doubled, and local church graveyards became overcrowded to the extent that disease was spreading and drinking water contaminated. The Burial Act of 1852 ordered seven new cemeteries to be built on the outskirts of London, and closed all metropolitan graveyards to new burials.

Long closed to burials, the old part of Nunhead Cemetery was for years neglected and unloved, but it's now a destination: a Local Nature Reserve, beloved of dog walkers and birdwatchers or just for gawping at our Victorian ancestors' love of over-the-top memorials. This is thanks in no small part to the Friends of Nunhead Cemetery, who since 1981 have helped raise funds to restore the chapel, and now the Grade II-listed East Lodge, and whose volunteers continue to undertake practical conservation work. On the last Sunday of every month at 2 p.m. they conduct tours of the cemetery's treasures (fonc.org.uk).

Among them is the Grade II-listed 'Scottish Political Martyrs' memorial: inspired by the French Revolution to campaign for greater democracy, they were transported to Australia for sedition for their pains. There are also many First and Second World War Commonwealth war graves and memorials.

roundabout. Here take the first right along Linden Grove to the main entrance of Nunhead Cemetery.

Follow the cemetery's central avenue to the chapel, and from there take the path climbing to your right. This takes you to the highest point of the cemetery, and eventually rewards you with a view of St Paul's Cathedral. Retrace your steps to the chapel and then follow the route of the Green Chain Walk downhill.

At the Limesford Gate turn left into

Limesford Road. When you reach the Waverley Arms, a nice pub, on the corner, turn right into Ivydale Road and continue on it until you hit the junction with Kelvington Road, where you turn left. This leads you into the tree-lined Brenchley Gardens, at the edge of One Tree Hill and Honor Oak. The park that runs alongside incorporates the track bed of the Crystal Palace High Level Railway that closed in 1954. Cross the road and head along Brenchley Gardens uphill to the right, and look out for a footpath on your left signposted 'Green Chain Walk and One Tree Hill'.

Now we have our second steep climb, this time a bosky one up woodland steps through One Tree Hill nature reserve. At the summit you'll find the 'Honor Oak' of legend. Though the current oak tree, as the plaque explains, was only planted in 1905, the story goes that a predecessor had the 'honour' of shading a resting Queen Elizabeth 1 when she was passing through in 1602.

Follow the ridge along the summit to an octagonal concrete platform, which operates as a viewpoint. This was built in 1916 as a mount for a Royal Navy gun used to defend London from bombing raids

One Tree Hill – Citizen Action

The name One Tree Hill apparently dates from when the hill was cleared of trees in the late nineteenth century, and all that remained was the Royal Oak. The wood that stood here had been one of the last bastions of the Great North Wood, an ancient woodland that had stretched across the hills and commons of South London, but been gradually eroded by the spread of London's suburbs.

The clearing of the hill was for the development of a private golf course, and it led to mass demonstrations and occupation lasting several years, and on some days attracting up to 10,000 angry protesters. This 'agitation' eventually led in 1905 to the London County Council purchasing the land and declaring it a public space.

The Royal Oak.

Betjeman's favourite view of London: from the viewpoint at One Tree Hill.

by German Zeppelin airships during the First World War. It was also here, on top of One Tree Hill, back in the late eighteenth century, that the East India Company had a semaphore telegraph station and a beacon to signal the arrival of its ships in the Thames. As the Napoleonic Wars reached their climax the station was commandeered by the Admiralty but did not feature in any of their telegraph lines. Beacons have continued to be lit here, to celebrate the coronation in 1952 of

Queen Elizabeth II, and all her subsequent jubilees.

The view between the trees west- and north-westwards is splendid, stretching as far as Alexandra Palace and Hampstead Heath on the horizon, with St Paul's and the City in the foreground. In 1957 Sir John Betjeman reported that One Tree Hill had a view 'that was better than that of Parliament Hill'.

To leave the viewpoint take the path immediately behind you as you're contemplating the view, and follow it downhill through the trees past St Augustine's Church all the way to Forest Hill Road at the bottom. If you want to finish the walk here, or just stop for refreshments, then turn left and you'll find Honor Oak Overground Station and several cafés and eateries. Alternatively, turn right to continue up to Forest Hill. (The name pays further note to the Great North Wood that used to coat these parts.)

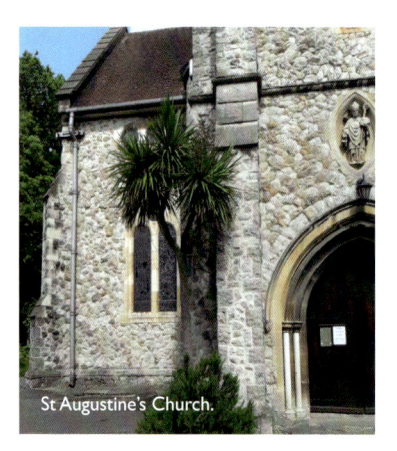

The residential roads we're now

St Augustine's Church.

Dawson Heights

A large social housing estate of 296 flats built in East Dulwich between 1968 and 1972, Dawson Heights was designed by the modernist architect Kate Macintosh, a champion of social housing. Despite its dominating presence in the landscape – part *ghat* on the Ganges, part Italian hill village – the estate has so far failed to be listed.

The Wembley Arch beyond Dawson Heights.

Telegraphs, Beacons and Masts

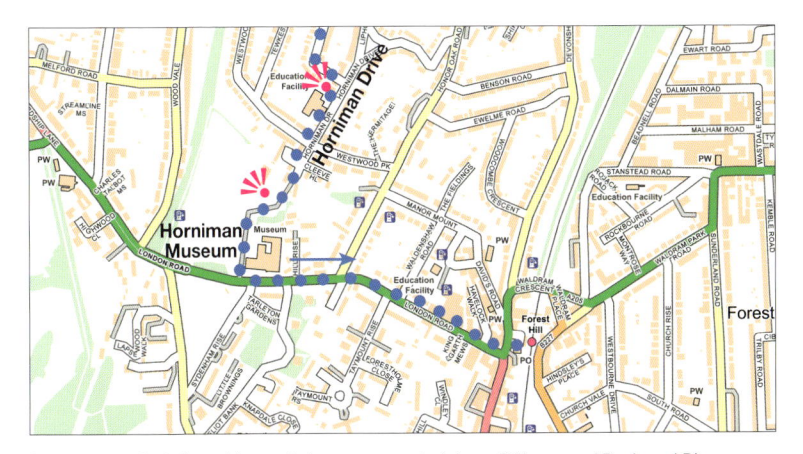

following to climb from Honor Oak up to Forest Hill could even be called the Forest Hill Alps, so dramatically hilly are they. Cross Forest Hill Road and, as you walk downhill, views of the new high-rise development at Nine Elms over on the south bank of the Thames, including the American Embassy among a forest of tower blocks of exclusive flats, begin to open out. Turn left onto Canonbie Road and you'll begin to climb again.

As the road steepens, make sure to keep looking behind you to admire the ever-expanding view as you ascend to the heights of Westwood Park and Ringmore Rise before reaching the apogee of the Alps in Horniman Drive. The whole drama of London unfolds, from the City round to Battersea Power Station and Wembley Stadium. The extraordinary, castle-like modernist estate that takes centre stage in the foreground is Dawson Heights.

At the top of Horniman Drive, the highest point on Forest Hill, is the Forest Hill Radio Station. Its origins are a bit mysterious, but apparently it is now a tetra mast, part of the communications network of the police and other emergency services.

Continue along the road past the mast, to the crossroad junction with Westwood Hill. You are now at the top of the ridge, and views abound on all sides – to the east, Shooters Hill and Eltham, while you

New Cross Gate to Forest Hill 85

might see the Crystal Palace transmitter popping up between the houses, some of which are quite lovely to behold, including an Art Deco gem built to resemble a ship, apparently with three terraces and views to die for.

A short step along the road is the rear entrance of the Horniman Museum and Gardens. You'll find yourself at the back of the Butterfly House and Animal Walk – goats, chickens and more, and all a bit unexpected – but turn the corner to the bandstand and terrace and another full-city panorama is upon you: the Shard and St Paul's Cathedral peeking over the leafy canopy bordering the sweeping parkland below the terrace, and Dawson Heights again dominating the foreground.

From Horniman Museum there is one hill left – downhill, down London Road, to Forest Hill Overground and British Rail station.

Horniman Museum

Opened in 1901 to house the collection of the nineteenth-century tea merchant Frederick Horniman's anthropological artifacts, this Grade II-listed museum was designed by Charles Harrison Townsend (who also designed Whitechapel Gallery and the Bishopsgate Institute) in his unique Arts and Crafts style.

It now houses one of the most significant ethnographic collections in the UK – some 80,000 objects from around the world – as well as a comprehensive musical instrument and natural world collection. Interactivity with animals, plants and objects is encouraged.

While Frederick Horniman was a great liberal social reformer, the museum doesn't shy away from the colonial and anachronistic associations of the collection, working with international partners and the community to ensure their cultural heritage is displayed and cared for respectfully. In November 2022 the museum returned six looted Benin Bronzes to Nigeria.

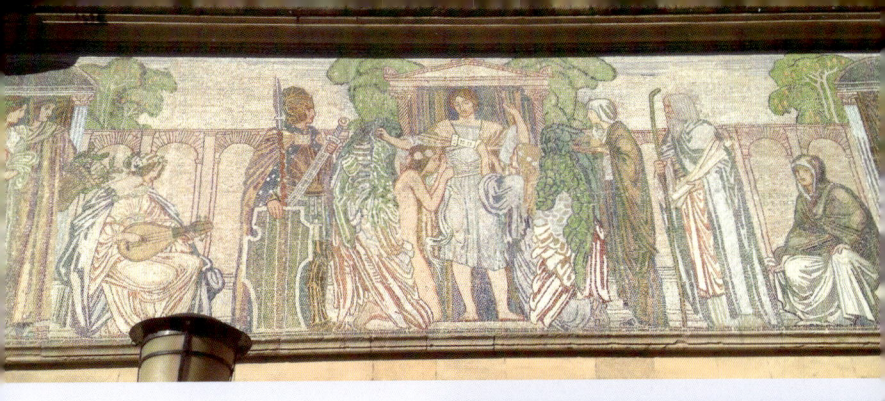

The beautiful gardens are themselves evolving collections, from the sunken formal garden designed in the 1930s to the recent medicinal and grassland gardens. Trees vary from soaring redwoods to majestic copper beech.

The stunning glasshouse near the café was transported from its original home as the conservatory at the Hornimans' Croydon mansion, Coombe Cliff (see p. 95).

Voted the Art Fund's Museum of the Year in 2022, the Horniman is a joyous place to visit – and free.

Crystal Palace

Summit: Sydenham Hill, 112 metres – 15th highest point in London
Start: Crystal Palace (Overground and National Rail), Penge West (Overground and National Rail), Sydenham Hill (National Rail)

The ridge on which the Crystal Palace stood has Sydenham Hill at one side and Westow Hill at the other. These days the Crystal Palace transmitter – probably the most recognisable hilltop landmark in south London – sits at the summit, at the eastern edge of what is now Crystal Palace Park.

In 1854 this was chosen as the permanent home for the 'Crystal Palace' glasshouse, the centrepiece of the 1851 Great Exhibition in Hyde Park, a celebration of Victorian industrial and cultural might.

The size of three St Paul's Cathedrals, it was designed by Joseph Paxton, already celebrated for his glasshouse work at Chatsworth for the Duke of Devonshire. These epic conservatories, constructed of wrought iron and the newly invented plate glass, were the pinnacle of innovation: the Window Tax had only just been repealed, and so much glass was unusual to the mid-nineteenth-century eye. It was a huge success.

The Crystal Palace sat in stately splendour at the top of Sydenham Hill, surrounded by Paxton's specially created terraces and stairways complete with sphinxes, many of which are now restored.

Television transmitters

The Crystal Palace Transmitting Station is the eighth tallest structure in London, and at 219 metres was the highest until 1990, when surpassed by One Canada Square at Canary Wharf. Built on the ruins of the Crystal Palace aquarium, it began transmitting in 1956, taking over from Alexandra Palace as the main BBC broadcast transmitter for the south of England.

The digital switchover in 2012 enabled Channel 4, ITV and Channel 5 to be added to the roster of channels. Previously these had been handled by the companion Croydon Transmitter, built in 1962 further along the ridge at Beaulieu Heights and now primarily used as back-up for Crystal Palace.

For over 80 years it was a major exhibition and entertainment venue for circuses, art shows, musical events, theatre and an aquarium. It hosted the world's first cat show in 1871, the first national motor show, the Festival of Empire in 1911, and after the war became the first home of the Imperial War Museum.

All this ended abruptly in 1936 when fire broke out, and within hours the entire structure was destroyed.

The Crystal Palace was built ten years earlier than Alexandra Palace (see p. 17), and it's interesting to compare the fortunes of these two Victorian pleasure domes, situated on high hills on opposite sides of London, whose transmitters heralded the twentieth-century communications boom. Alexandra Palace survives; the Crystal Palace is a vanished wonder.

The sweeping park that cascades downhill from the Crystal Palace terraces was also a showcase for new horticultural design ideas. George Thomson introduced six new flowerbeds coloured as different species of butterflies. Edward Milner designed the Italian gardens, fountains, and the great maze (now restored).

But most extraordinary of all were Benjamin Waterhouse Hawkins' dinosaur sculptures, based on 33 recent fossil discoveries – a sensation then and still today as you spy them amid the undergrowth. Today the park is Grade II listed.

The avenue of cherry trees leading up through Park Hill Gardens.

6

Seven Hills of Croydon

East Croydon to New Addington

When Croydon was being redeveloped during the Sixties, the story goes, Birmingham, with its ring road and Bull Ring, had already surrounded its city centre with six multi-storey car parks. So Croydon, its planners were determined, envisioning a utopia of flyovers, underpasses and the biggest shopping mall in the South-East, had to go one better … Seven multi-storeys were duly built around the new, high-rise town centre, and became known as the 'Seven Hills of Croydon'.

This walk is most definitely not about the car parks but rather the actual ridge of hills leading roughly east, of which there are indeed seven to climb, several among the highest in London.

This is a longish walk that will surprise, even amaze, anyone who had written off Croydon as a concrete jungle, by revealing its many surprising facets: heathland, ancient woodland, sweeping parkland, and the formal gardens of grand country houses. For much of it you'll feel as though you're out in the countryside.

Summits:
Coombe Park, 90m
Addington Hills viewpoint, 142m – 7th highest point in London
Bramley Bank, 140m
Littleheath Woods, 160m – 3rd highest point in London
(Sanderstead Plantation, 175m – 2nd highest point in London)
Selsdon Wood, 135m
Frith Wood, 155m
New Addington, 150m

Length: 7 miles – 11 km
Time: 4 hours
Total ascent: 951 feet – 290 metres
Start: East Croydon Station – British Rail and Tramlink
Finish: New Addington Tramlink stop
Base camp: Cafés at East Croydon Station; also in Park Hill Gardens, Lloyd Park and Coombe Wood Gardens.

Come out of the front of East Croydon Station and cross the tram tracks (first looking carefully in both directions) and the road to reach Altyre Road opposite, to the left of the railway bridge. (Croydon is one of only seven towns in the country to have a tram system, and the only one in the south of the country.)

To your left, the octagonal white tower built as NLA House, and now known as No. 1 Croydon, was designed by Richard Seifert, also the architect of Centre Point on Tottenham Court Road, and is the most striking symptom of the attempt during the Sixties to transform Croydon into a 'mini-Manhattan', a story fascinatingly told

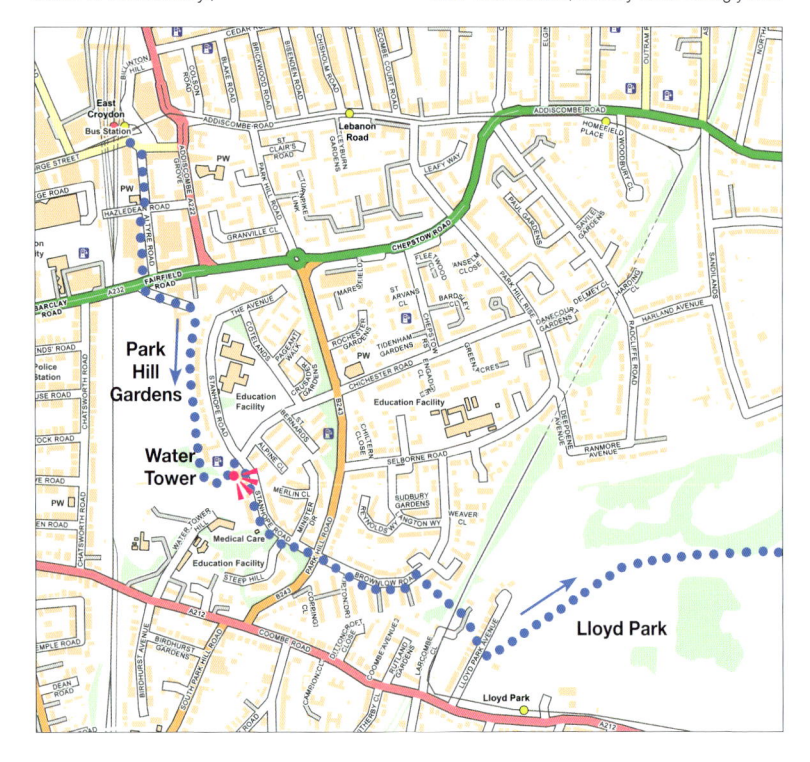

92 Seven Hills of Croydon

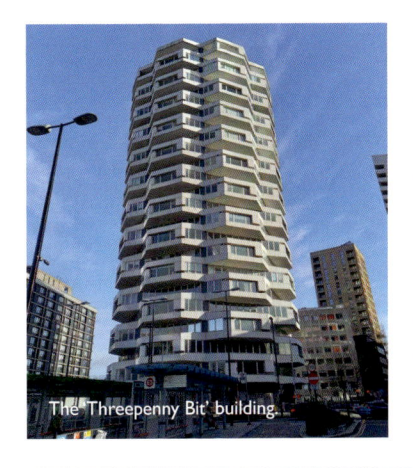

by John Grindrod (who grew up in New Addington) in *Concretopia*. In pre-decimal times it was nicknamed 'the Threepenny Bit' building, and has since been compared to a stack of 50p pieces.

Walk up Altyre Road, past the large hole to your right where one of Croydon's Seven Hills, the Fairfield multi-storey car park, used to stand. In 1995 the law courts just round the corner played host to the celebrated trial of the footballer Eric Cantona, charged with launching

The 'Threepenny Bit' building.

The Seven Hills of Croydon

Six of Croydon's original seven multi-storey car parks survive: Dingwall Road, Allders, Whitgift Centre, Tamworth Road/Centrale, Surrey Street and Wandle Road. The seventh, Fairfield, shown here to the rear of the Fairfield Halls concert hall, has been demolished. It was in the Nineties that the architect Nigel Coates likened them to the Seven Hills of Rome, and for ten years Vincent Lacovara of Croydon Council led guided tours of them.

a kung-fu kick at a home supporter during Crystal Palace vs Manchester United game at Selhurst Park to the north of Croydon. Cross the main road and enter Park Hill Gardens immediately opposite. Park Hill is our first ascent.

Already, within minutes of leaving the forest of skyscrapers around the railway station, you find yourself in the first of Croydon's many and substantial tracts of green space. This is a town built right on the edge of London's Green Belt, and we shall soon find ourselves out in it. Follow the cherry tree-lined path as it climbs gently upwards towards the water tower, a local landmark. To your right, as the glinting skyline of central Croydon unfolds, you'll start to see the valley in which Croydon was built.

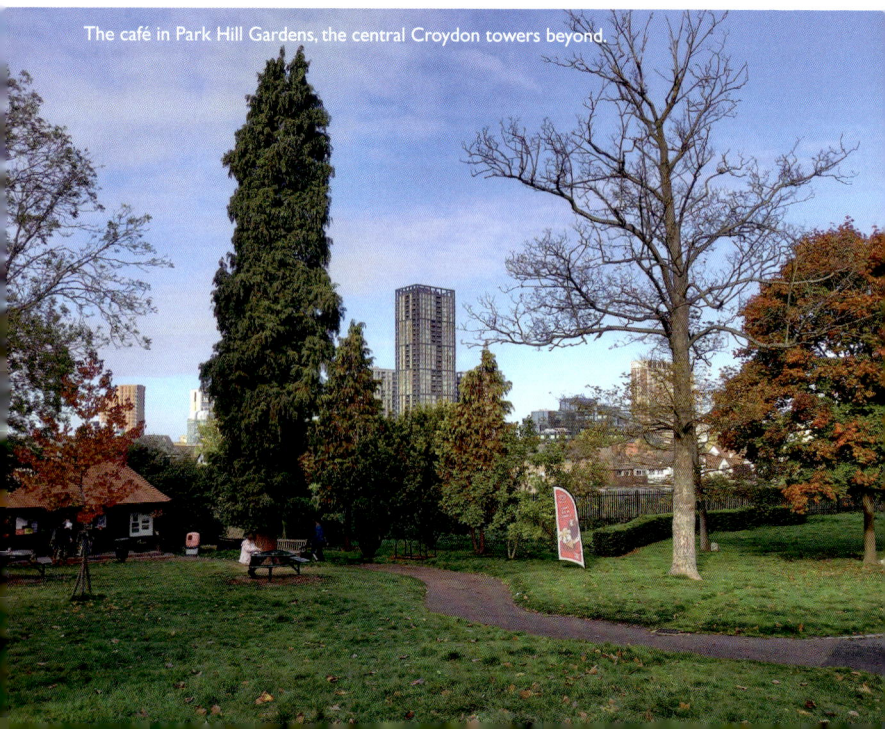

The Croydon skyline reaching ever higher.

The café in Park Hill Gardens, the central Croydon towers beyond.

The path up through Lloyd Park.

At the water tower you'll take the path to the left, but beforehand you might want to explore the walled garden on the far side of the park. Currently undergoing restoration, it was once part of Coombe Cliff House (surviving behind it as a school), and laid out by the Horniman family, tea importers and founders of the Horniman Museum at Forest Hill. In 1987 the ornate conservatory of Coombe Cliff House was transplanted to become a striking adjunct to the museum. The garden also celebrates Cicely Mary Barker, Croydon resident and illustrator of the Flower Fairy books.

Leave the park beyond the water tower to emerge into Stanhope Road. Turn right: ahead of you is the first view of the Addington Hills and the spire of Royal Russell School's chapel. At the bottom of the road cross Park Hill Road into Brownlow Road, and then turn right onto Fairfield Path, which is signposted as part of the Vanguard Way, a 66-mile (106 km) walking route from East Croydon to Newhaven on the south coast. Eventually the path ducks under the tram tracks, and you'll come to Lloyd Park.

This huge swathe of mostly open parkland is named after Frank Lloyd, a newspaper magnate of the early twentieth century whose long-forgotten newspapers included the *Sunday News* and the *Daily Chronicle*, and who lived on the edge of it in Coombe House, now a school. Upon his death in 1927 he bequeathed the land to create this park. To visit the café and facilities, turn left and take the park's perimeter path – easy to spot.

Otherwise, we start our second climb, taking the main path as it gently ascends across the greensward and bends to the right. Turn right along the edge of the woodland – you'll notice the baskets of the Disc Golf course spreading out below you on your right – keeping an eye out for a gap in the hedge ahead of you at the end of the Disc Golf course, which leads into

East Croydon to New Addington 95

Coombe Park. Take a course across the parkland aiming for the far corner, past the lone oak tree and towards the rugby and football goals, then exit through the yellow metal gate into Coombe Farm Lane. Go straight ahead, and then bear right towards Oaks Road. Don't be tempted to turn left towards the sports grounds and car park. When you reach the road a thatched cottage, 80 Oaks Road should be on your left.

Turn right towards the traffic lights and cross first the tram line (look carefully both ways first) and then Coombe Road – cars come down the hill fast here, so be sure to make use of the central reservation slightly further up. On the corner you will see Coombe Wood Gardens with a popular café. This was once also the stables for the council's park rangers, who patrolled on horseback; they're now the toilets.

Now retrace your steps back across the tram line, past the car park and opposite Coombe Farm Lane take the path to the right that ascends through the trees. You are now officially in the Addington Hills.

We climb steadily uphill along a classic heathland ridge, sandy underfoot and

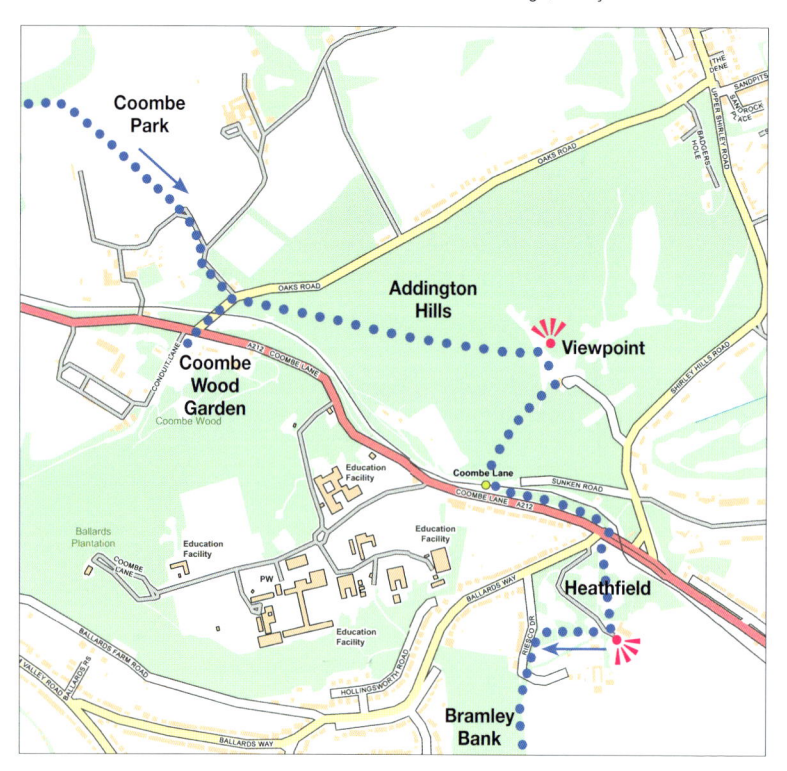

Coombe Wood Gardens

Coombe Wood Gardens belonged to Coombe Wood House, a substantial house in the late-Victorian half-timbered style built in 1898 and once owned by Arthur Lloyd, the brother of Frank of Lloyd Park fame. Until recently it was a restaurant, and you'll catch sight of it as you walk through the gardens. These splendid 14 acres of woodland gardens were opened to the public in 1948, when the house became a convalescence home attached to Croydon General Hospital.

At the entrance is the impressive Baron's Pond, which is fed by two natural streams, one of which tumbles over a waterfall. The bordering rockery is made using Pulhamite, an artificial stone developed by James Pulham & Son, a well-reputed landscaping firm of the late nineteenth century.

Despite the ravages of time the gardens have stayed true to their original Victorian design. The hedge-lined paths encourage you to wander through a series of seasonally themed garden rooms sculpted against a backdrop of mature woodland. The Winter Garden is crammed with heathers. In late spring the woodlands are alive with the vibrant hues of rhododendrons and azaleas; in summer it's the turn of the rose garden, and in the autumn foliage and grasses provide stunning colour.

full of spiky gorse, following the path as it dips down and then up again. (At the far end of the ridge, the venerable Addington Golf Club, which used to number Croydon resident Ronnie Corbett among its members, is considered one of the finest classic heathland courses in the country.) Proceed down some steps, across a valley wooded with beech trees, and up another flight of steps. The ground then plateaus, before another flight of steps takes us down, and then one more up across another gully. At the top of these last steps you should climb out beside the Addington Hills viewpoint.

Here, at a height of 140 metres, a substantial stone-built platform commands a stunning view: the panoramic skyline stretches from Canary Wharf and London Docklands to the right, across to the City, the Shard, the Crystal Palace Transmitter mast, the Croydon Transmitter mast, the bulbous bulk of the One Blackfriars office tower, the Wembley Arch, and the distant hills of North-West London. In the foreground are St Helier Hospital (the white edifice to the left), and central Croydon, and especially the eye-smacking purple-and-red Saffron Tower. Who'd have thought it of Croydon?

Addington Hills

Named after the nearby ancient parish of Addington, the hills were once an area called Pripledeane, 'gravel valley' in Middle English. Until the nineteenth century the extraction of gravel had been a thriving industry in the area, and the road running up from Addington is still called Gravel Hill. During the eighteenth century Addington Cricket Club, a top club of the day, played their matches up on the hills.

Addington Hills now covers 130 acres of woods and heathland, created from land either donated or purchased by the Croydon Board of Health. In 1903 Frank Lloyd of Coombe Park fame donated the birch wood on its west side.

The path up through the Addington Hills.

When I first did this walk in spring 2022 the heath directly beyond the viewpoint was a glorious riot of yellow flowering gorse. Sadly, that summer the drought saw fires rampage through the area, and a subsequent visit revealed the charred devastation. Hopefully by the time you pass through the gorse will have regenerated.

From the viewing platform follow the London Loop path until you reach the Royal Garden restaurant. Turn right here and follow the London Loop sign labelled 'Selsdon Wood'. Keep bearing left after about 100 metres as the path forks, and then keep left again at the large dead tree until you come out at the Coombe Lane tram stop. If you want to finish the walk here you can catch the tram from the other platform back to East Croydon.

Cross the tram tracks carefully and follow the London Loop signs left along Coombe Lane, noting another water tower on the left. Cross at the lights and turn left into Heathfield. Immediately after the Lodge turn left onto a woodland walk and head downhill to the pond and Heathfield House, a Georgian villa built in the late eighteenth century. Behind it you'll find a picturesque, Italianate terrace from which the land falls away towards Addington. The main road to the left is Gravel Hill.

The lovely grounds at Heathfield feature a fine Giant Redwood and other specimen trees, and the walled garden is an oasis of calm. Behind it is the Croydon Ecology Centre. At the time of writing, however, access to the house and grounds, which were acquired for the people of Croydon in the 1960s, is under threat, as the borough tries to fend off its current financial crisis. Should this come to pass, there is an alternative route. Instead of entering Heathfield, follow Ballard's Way from the traffic lights mentioned above and

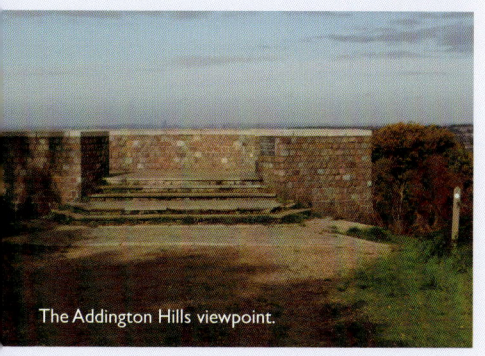

The Croydon skyline from the viewpoint.

The Addington Hills viewpoint.

East Croydon to New Addington 99

Heathfield house.

The Italian terrace.

turn left into Riesco Drive.

After a detour around Heathfield garden, follow the path around the pond and up steps to emerge in the car park.

Turn left back into Riesco Drive and follow it down to the end, past a rustic cottage, to enter the London Wildlife Trust's Bramley Bank Nature Reserve. Follow the path

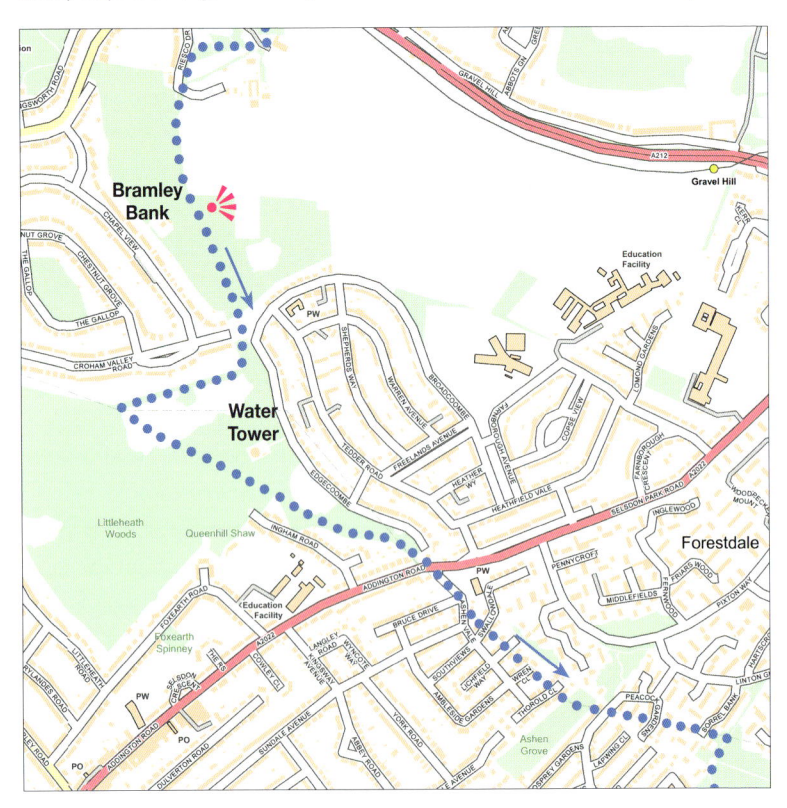

The Trojan Car Company
A brass plaque on the Addington Hills viewpoint reveals that the land to build it on was donated in 1963 by Alderman Basil Monk, a director of the Croydon-based Trojan Car Company, located on Purley Way near the old Croydon Aerodrome. Among the vehicles it manufactured was the Trojan 200 bubble car.

through the wood with bucolic views to your left of countryside and fields of livestock. Now we've reached the edge of the Green Belt, and left the heathland terrain behind.

The path descends to come out on a small open space that separates two housing estates – oddly not connected by road. To the left is Monk's Hill, to the right Ballard's Farm. This was previously the site of a dairy farm, whose lush, rolling countryside apparently gained it the nickname 'Little Devon'.

Turn right into Littleheath Wood, and pick up the London Loop path again through open grassland named Fallen Oak Field. Though it might seem as if the Addington Hills viewpoint was the highest point of our walk, at the top of this wood we'll have reached 160 metres. To the left you'll see yet another water tower poking through the trees, and to your right the spire of Royal Russell School Chapel. This was built in 1921 as a war memorial to the Great War and decorated by the now discredited artist, Eric Gill. Among Royal Russell's alumni is the actor Martin Clunes. Take the left fork underneath a line of electricity pylons to head for some fallen logs at the edge of the trees.

Turn left up – fourth hill! – onto the Vanguard Way through the wood, with the water tower immediately on your left. At the top the path heads downhill again. Turn right and continue your descent among deciduous trees through bluebell woods, until the path comes out on the Addington Road.

Should you want refreshments, to your right the Addington Road will bring you after a quarter of mile to the centre of Selsdon. Continue beyond the traffic lights and, completists might like to know, on the right you'll reach the second highest point in Greater London, within Sanderstead Plantation. It's a remarkably unprepossessing peak, affording no views and reached by an almost imperceptible incline, so not on our route. If you want to finish your walk here, the 64 bus will take you to Addington Village for the tram or (the other direction) all the

East Croydon to New Addington 101

way back to Croydon.

Otherwise, cross busy Addington Road by the pelican crossing to Ashen Vale and take the path to the left alongside the Mormon church. Cross the road, then cross Peacock Gardens and follow the path uphill into Selsdon Wood, a fine ancient woodland rich in fauna, including a pair of white squirrels, last seen in 2021,

Wood anemones in Selsdon Wood.

and 42 species of trees, and another nature reserve, this time owned by the National Trust. Follow Addington Corner Path, which is also part of the London Loop, through the woods, which in the spring

In late spring bluebells carpet Selsdon Wood and Frith Wood.

102 Seven Hills of Croydon

are the finest place anywhere in London to see white wood anemones.

You come out of Selsdon Wood by the end of Courtwood Lane, where you can also catch a bus back to Croydon. Take the bridleway opposite for another uphill climb – the sixth of our seven – with the undulating sweep of Farleigh Court golf course on the right. At the left fork follow the path along the fence – Bears Wood scout campsite is on the other side – taking care not to trip in one of the badger setts that have cratered the path. You are now in Frith Wood, which in late spring is resplendent with bluebells. On your left is another golf course, Addington Court.

Turn left onto Tandridge Border Path, which follows the boundary line of the county of Surrey – we are right on the very edge of Greater London. The path descends through the wood to come out on Featherbed Lane. Cross the road and take the path immediately opposite to haul up our final climb into New Addington, a huge post-war housing development begun as a slum clearance project that now covers some thousand acres and has a population of over 20,000. After all these miles walking among woods, heathland and rolling fields we suddenly find ourselves in what is virtually a small town isolated up on the hill.

At Fishers Farm Amenity Centre turn right into North Downs Road and then dogleg left into Overbury Crescent. At the end of the road, you'll find the New Addington tram terminus for the tram to whizz you up and down all those hills back to East Croydon in just 20 minutes.

The path alongside Frith Wood.

Water Towers

They spring up all over London, sometimes hidden among suburban streets, sometimes as dominant landmarks on the horizon. Evolving in the early Victorian era in response to the demand for a reliable water supply, they were able to store water to be released when needed. The tower's height meant the water could be pumped from the storage tank by hydrostatic pressure, gravity forcing it downwards and into the local water supply.

And this is the reason water towers are a looming presence on the landscape on this book's walks. To maximise the height and pressure advantage, water towers were often located on hills, as well as close to or above underground reservoir systems.

Since water supply was in private ownership until the beginning of the twentieth century there was no universal design for these towers, which led to the idiosyncratic, eclectic and sometimes downright eccentric architecture you find. Most of the older water towers are now disused, technology and age having rendered them superfluous, but they are a wonderful reminder of the creativity that was employed in our industrial heritage.

Water towers you might meet on your walk:

Grade II-listed

Shooters Hill water tower, built in 1910, is an octagonal brick tower with pointed tile roof and rounded arched openings. It dominates the landscape like a Romanesque church tower.

Croydon water tower in Park Hill was built in 1867, and has a crenelated top like a fantasy Norman castle keep. The tower boasts a viewing gallery which in the Victorian age was a local tourist attraction. At the time of writing it was covered in scaffolding and undergoing restoration.

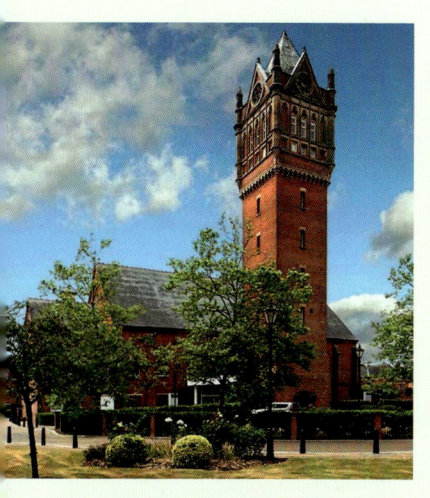

Landmark Tower, Woodford Green was built as the water tower for Claybury Hospital, a Victorian asylum, and is now a luxury three-bedroom house. Its High Gothic architecture is reminiscent of Big Ben and St Pancras Station, and can be seen for miles around across North and East London.

Later water towers

Havering-atte-Bower water tower was constructed out of reinforced concrete in 1931. A Norman-style tower that looks as if it has been modelled on the chateau at Falaise, its more prosaic function was to help with the water pressure in Romford.

Addington Hills water tower, Croydon. Certainly the ugly sister here, this boxy Modernist concrete water tower shouts twentieth century – no historic pretence.

Littleheath water tower, Croydon. A big, white, 1950s, circular spaceship hidden among the trees that hovers over the surrounding countryside.

Water Towers 105

The Thames from Richmond Hill.

⑦

A Royal Park and a Commoner Common

Richmond to Wimbledon

This long and amiable ramble across south-west London joins two of London's most treasured green lungs, Richmond Park and Wimbledon Common, that form part of a plateau above the River Thames. The summits – huge, level plains – are therefore not the scenic highlight: the finest views are to be had on the initial climb and the final descent (unusually, a residential suburban street), but there are more along the way, as well as some beautiful gardens and a notable plantation.

The whole route is quite a long one, but you can make it into a shorter Richmond circular of a couple of hours. Paths designated as 'Rides' – i.e. designated as suitable for horse riding – may be muddy in winter or dusty in summer.

Summits:
King Henry's Mound, Richmond Park, 56m
Wimbledon Common, 51m

Length: 8 miles – 13 kilometres (4 miles – 6.3 kilometres via circular shortcut)
Time: 4½ hours (2 hours via circular shortcut)
Total ascent: 435 feet – 132 metre
Start: Richmond Station – British Rail, Overground and District Line
Finish: Wimbledon Station – British Rail, District Line and Tramlink
Base camp: Abundant refreshment opportunities in both Richmond and Wimbledon (village and town centre); Richmond Park.

Turn left out of Richmond Station into the Quadrant and Richmond town centre – plenty of coffee shops and eateries here for all tastes. Arguably the nicest coffee shops are further on towards Richmond Hill.

Cross at the traffic lights to head up George Street, and bear left into Hill Street. Already our route is beginning to climb. Hill Street becomes Hill Rise and eventually Richmond Hill. Richmond Hill the neighbourhood is one of London's most exclusive: Mick Jagger is one of its residents, and a couple of years ago tweeted a picture of himself with his favourite tree in Richmond Park.

At Richmond Hill Court cross to the right-hand pavement – here you will find

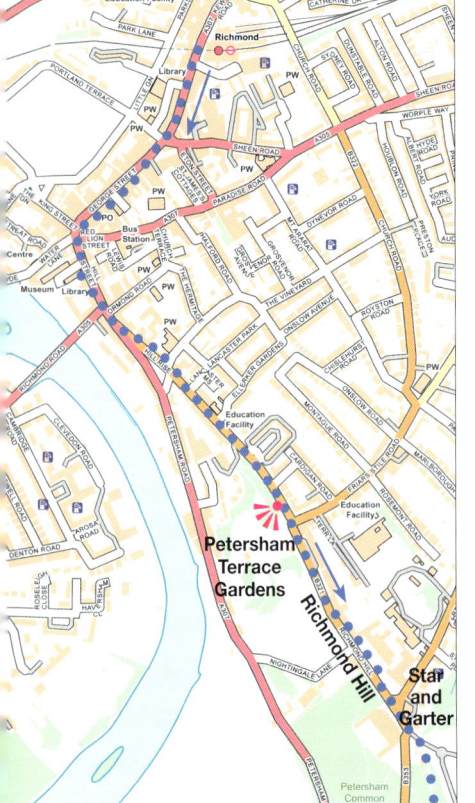

Twickenham Stadium with plane approaching, from Richmond Hill.

Terrace Walk and Cardigan Gate, the first entrance to Petersham Terrace Gardens.

As you continue along Terrace Walk you'll come upon your first memorable view of the day: a stunning prospect

108 A Royal Park and a Commoner Common

Petersham Terrace Gardens

These tree-fringed, ornamental gardens, which slope all the way down to Petersham Meadows in the Thames flood plain, were developed by the 5th Duke of Buccleuch as part of his estate. Following his death they were put up for sale and purchased by the Richmond vestry, and in 1887 opened to the public. In 1926 the gardens were extended when Richmond Council purchased more land. A major restoration programme in the noughties has revitalised the gardens to create a lush oasis. The design includes a mixture of sustainable planting, which as well as being attractive is valuable to wildlife as well as the more traditional planting of rose gardens and herbaceous borders.

down to the River Thames and across to the distant hills towards Windsor. Where many of the great views to be had in this book's other walks are of the capital's ever-more powerhouse skyline, this one is distinguished by the limpid prospect of the famous water meadows beneath – and all available just a few minutes' climb from the end of a Tube line.

The view is protected by an Act of Parliament passed in 1902, and protects the land sweeping down to the river from development as well as the views. The centrepiece of the river view is Glover's Island, which is also protected and owned by Richmond Council. To the

Petersham Meadows sweeping down to the Thames.

right the enormous, cantilevered oval is Twickenham rugby stadium, above which you'll see planes following each other in on their final descent into Heathrow.

Carry on up the hill past the Richmond Hill Hotel, and cross the road at the

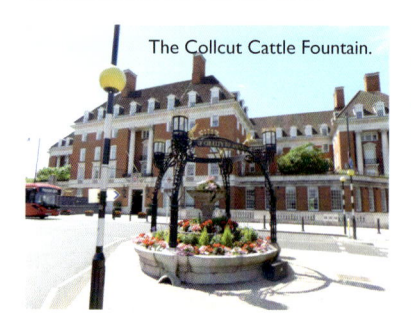

The Collcut Cattle Fountain.

roundabout. The memorial dominating the roundabout is known as the Collcutt Cattle Fountain. It was commissioned to commemorate the work of the local RSPCA, and designed by the Victorian Arts and Crafts architect T. E. Collcutt. Recent conservation work on this Grade II-listed monument was undertaken by the Richmond Society.

Continue along left-hand path opposite the Star and Garter building on your right. Now converted into flats, the striking Star and Garter building was built in 1924 as the Royal Star and Garter Home, based on plans by the eminent architect Sir Giles Gilbert Scott (of Battersea Power Station and Liverpool Cathedral fame), to provide accommodation and nursing for injured servicemen.

Richmond Gate takes you into Richmond Park.

Take the path to your right past the public toilets with the road to your left. Keep on this path until you come to a metal gate with a hut to the left. Ignore the gate, and instead turn and cross the road and follow the path immediately opposite with

Richmond Park

Richmond has been home to royal palaces since Tudor times, when Henry VII built his new palace on the Thames (destroyed during the English Civil War). However, it was Charles I who created the new deer park that would eventually become Richmond Park. A herd of red and

fallow deer remains in the park today. *Do NOT approach them; far less try to stroke or feed them. If you have a dog with you, it MUST be on a lead.*

The park passed through the hands of various royals and other notables who used it as their country estate. Queen Elizabeth II lived here briefly as a baby, at White Lodge, which is now home to the Royal Ballet School. Public access to the park was granted by Parliament in 1872. At 2,500 acres it is claimed to be the largest urban park in Europe, and it is designated a National Nature Reserve.

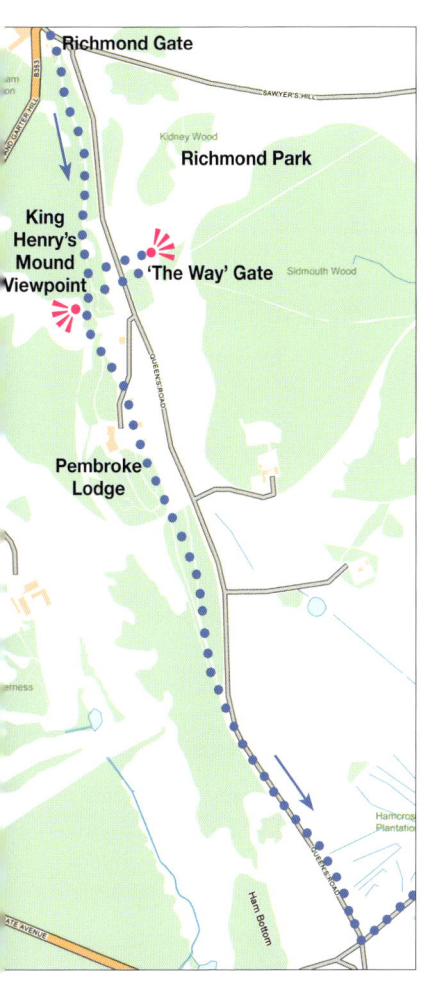

a view of the London skyline ahead. You should be able to see the BT Tower, the London Eye, the City and the Shard. Take the path to the right towards the side of a wooded area known as Sidmouth Woods, where you'll find ornate metal gates bearing the legend 'The Way'. These were erected to mark the tercentenary of St Paul's Cathedral in 2011.

Now walk back towards the road through the avenue of trees, turn towards the gates and you'll see the reason for those commemorative gates: an

King Henry's Mound

This Bronze Age burial chamber represents the highest point on Richmond Hill, and affords special views in both directions. On one side, to the east, is the protected vista of St Paul's Cathedral, and on the other, although hard to see with the naked eye, is Windsor Castle. There is a telescope theoretically offering magnified vision, but you might well find that bringing your own binoculars is the better option.

Though the 1902 Act of Parliament has indeed prevented any high-rise development between Richmond Park and the City obstructing the prospect of St Paul's, purists have argued that a recent skyscraper erected in Stratford further to the east has intruded into the untrammelled view from behind.

uninterrupted view of St Paul's. A line of posts marks it out. Once back at the road cross it and go through the gate opposite. To the right the hump among the trees is King Henry's Mound.

From King Henry's Mound take a path down to the left and wander through some immaculate formal gardens. Soon you'll find yourself at Pembroke Lodge, a Grade II-listed Georgian villa and the premier refreshment spot in Richmond Park, serving hot food, sandwiches, cakes and drinks. You can dine either inside or out on the magnificent terrace looking out to the west over the Thames. (There are more basic refreshment facilities, and more toilets, out in the car park.)

If one hill is enough for you then from here you can turn this into a circular walk via the following route downhill through Petersham Terrace Gardens back to Richmond. Once you continue into Richmond Park there are no other public transport options until you reach the A3, where buses (85 and 265) will connect you with Putney Station.

To continue the walk towards Wimbledon leave Pembroke Lodge through the car park, and take a path that leads to the right to walk parallel to the road. We're now crossing the broad plateau of Richmond Park before we descend its far side. You are aiming for the Isabella Plantation. At a crossroads take the left turn. In about 100 metres you'll see a tarmac path on the right which leads into

Shortcut back to Richmond

From the terrace of Pembroke Lodge take the path and steps down to the bottom of the grounds. Slightly to the left is a gate into Petersham Park. Follow the path straight ahead downhill. Turn right onto a wide gravel path. The church peeping through the trees on your left was once All Saints' Church, but this Grade II-listed building is now a private residence.

Exit at Petersham Gate (there are toilets on your left just inside the gate).

Cross the road and follow the footpath immediately opposite towards the river (there are signs for the Capital Ring here). Pass the graveyard for St Peter's Church and turn right into a lane. Keep following the footpath ahead into Petersham Meadows until you reach Eileen's Café, a highly rated and delightful converted public convenience at the corner of Buccleuch Gardens, which is open every day.

From the café continue through the gardens until you see Grotto Gate, which leads under the main road on your right and into Petersham Terrace Gardens. From here ascend the path past Hollyhock Café (also open every day) and up to Landsdown Gate on Richmond Hill. You should now recognise your surroundings from earlier. Turn left and retrace your steps downhill until you reach Richmond Station.

Isabella Plantation

This 40-acre Victorian woodland plantation was opened to the public in 1953, and is known for its azalea, rhododendron and camellia collection. These are at their best in spring and early summer, but there is plenty of year-round interest provided by native and exotic trees, shrubs and numerous ponds.

Richmond to Wimbledon

the plantation.

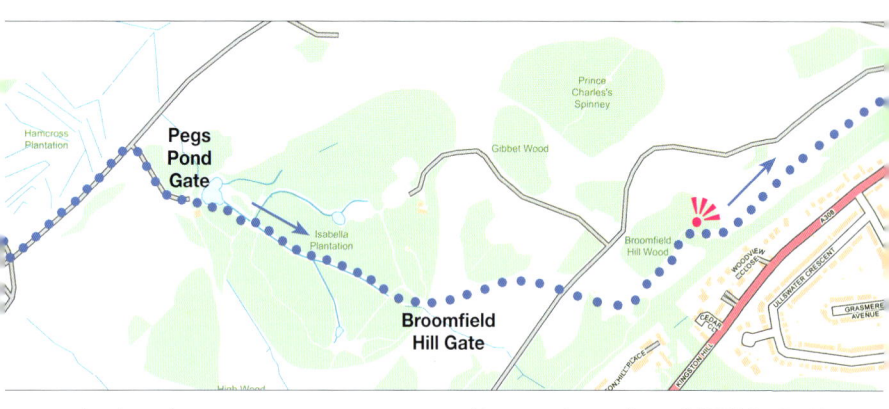

Enter the plantation at what is called Pegs Pond Gate. Take the path along the boardwalk and past Pegs Pond. Make your way to the exit point at Broomfield Hill Gate (there are signs to Broomfield Hill Car Park).

From Broomfield Hill Gate head straight uphill towards the car park. At the far end of the car park you'll see a path to the left. This will gradually open out views across to the City. The path gradually descends off the plateau until eventually you arrive at Robin Hood Gate and its pastoral riding stables. There are more toilets here, and also buses if you want to end the walk at this point.

At the Gate leave the park and cross the main A3 road at the lights.

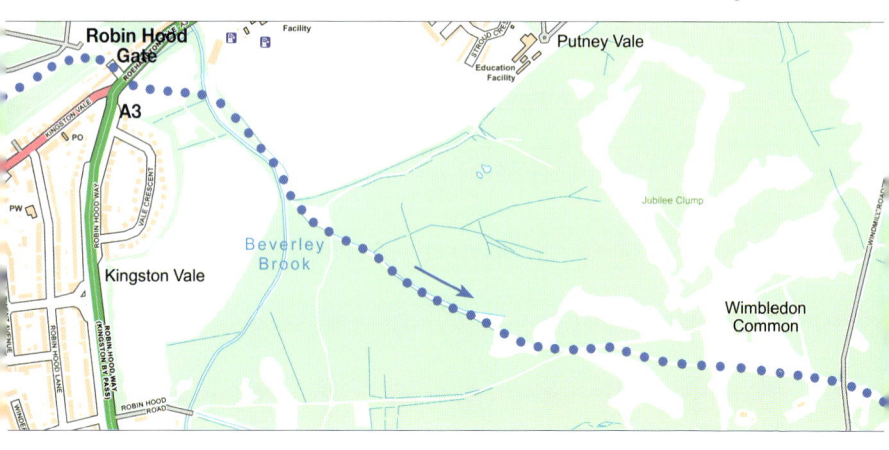

The descent from Broomfield Hill Gate to the A3.

114 A Royal Park and a Commoner Common

Wimbledon Common, with Wimbledon Village beyond.

Immediately opposite you'll find the entrance to what is the beginning of Wimbledon Common. Enter the parkland and continue along the path ahead, crossing a bridge and turning right along a wooded path. At a fork turn left, and left again at a second fork along a 'ride'.

Now we start to climb again, up

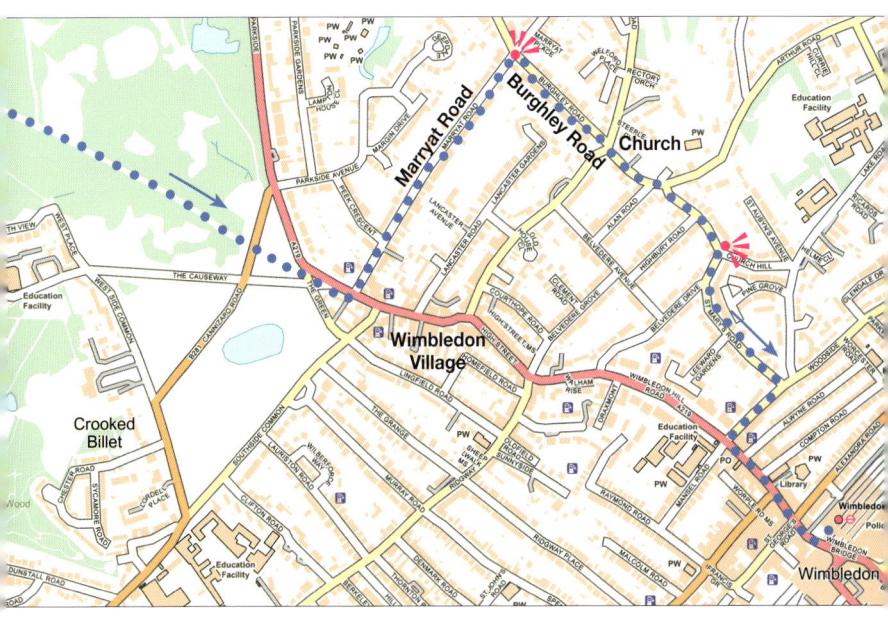

Richmond to Wimbledon 115

The City of London skyline from Marryat Road.

towards our second plateau. Keep left as you continue uphill; you'll see a golf course (London Scottish) on either side of the ride. Take the fork to the right and continue straight on until you reach a crossroads at the top of Wimbledon Hill. We've now reached the top of our second plateau, and once more you can gaze around you and wonder where the view went. Don't worry: it'll come. Follow the path waymarked 'The Causeway', and at the war memorial take the second right into Wimbledon Village and High Street.

The walk continues by turning left into Marryat Road, but first you might want to take a break at one of the numerous cafés, restaurants and pubs in the village.

Halfway down steep Marryat Road a splendid view begins to unfold: first Battersea Power Station, followed by the London Eye and, further along, the high-rise skyline of the City. Perhaps the only other place in Wimbledon that can rival this prospect of the city spread out ahead of you is Henman Hill (or Murray Mound) at the All-England Club, but there the window of opportunity is rather more circumscribed, and expensive.

Turn right into Burghley Road and then cross into St Mary's Road past St Mary's Church, designed in 1843 by George Gilbert Scott, of Albert Memorial and St Pancras Station Hotel fame (grandfather of Giles, whose work we encountered earlier). A notable mausoleum in the churchyard is of Sir Joseph Bazalgette, engineer extraordinaire and responsible for the construction of London's sewer

116 A Royal Park and a Commoner Common

system and the Thames embankments. Beside the entrance to the church is Stag Lodge, once the entrance lodge for Wimbledon Park House, which was demolished in 1949.

St Mary's Road continues our descent, with a last view: this time of Croydon and the Addington Hills visible in the distance – which we ascended in the previous walk. Turn right into Woodside and then left into Wimbledon Hill Road, which you can follow downhill back to Wimbledon Station.

The Croydon skyline from St Mary's Road.

Guinness Hills

Northala Hills (see p. 128) are not the first to use waste material to grace an unlovely stretch of the A40. The so-called 'Guinness Hills' were.

In 1936 the Guinness Brewery had opened at Park Royal, designed in magnificent modernist style by Alexander Gibb and Sir Giles Gilbert Scott, of Battersea Power Station renown. At its peak it was producing 1.6 million barrels a year, eight times more than any other brewery.

That it was built next to Hanger Lane – Hangr Hill is Anglo-Saxon for wooded slope – and Park Royal, originally a royal agricultural showground, was not lost on the Guinness management. Keen to foster a healthy co-existence between industry and nature, they created a 'garden city brewery': playing fields (hosting Olympic hockey in 1948) and a bowling green, as well as landscaped lawns and gardens and no fewer than 1,380 trees.

By the late 1950s plans for a four-lane highway and the Hangar Lane underpass where Western Avenue (A40) met the North Circular, outside the brewery gates, threatened this green oasis.

The elegant solution saw 20,000 tons of subsoil from the tunnel's excavation dumped in 1962 onto Guinness land opposite Park Royal Tube, and beautifully moulded, to the design of the distinguished landscape architect Geoffrey Jellicoe, whose projects include the Kennedy Memorial at Runnymede, into two 9 metre-high hillocks, screening the brewery from the thunderous traffic and framing it within the urban landscape.

At some point the Guinness Hills disappeared. Were they subsumed into further A40 road-widening in the 1990s, or did they make way for a Park Plaza hotel? In 2006, in what the Twentieth-Century Society condemned as 'pure architectural vandalism', the brewery itself was demolished.

The Guinness Hills beside the A40.

'The garden city brewery.'

Primrose Hill

Summit: 63m
Start: A choice of St John's Wood, Swiss Cottage or Chalk Farm Tube stations, via a short walk, or a longer and more scenic approach from Baker Street or Great Portland Street through Regent's Park

Just north of Regent's Park, to which it is connected by a footbridge over the canal, Primrose Hill is one of London's protected views of St Paul's. A Grade II-listed Royal Park in its own right, it has given its name to one of the fashionable 'London Villages' forever associated with a certain kind of Nineties celebrity glamour.

The dramatic panorama from the grassy summit includes the usual suspects, from the London Eye and BT Tower round to the Shard, and next to it a good view of Guy's Hospital, London's tallest building when it was built in 1974. But in the foreground are some rarer bird's-eye views: through the tree-fringed edge of the park you can see London Zoo and its iconic architecture – the Grade-II listed Mappin Terraces, designed in 1913, and Snowdon Aviary, designed in 1962 – as well as St Mark's Church on Prince Albert Road and, behind that St Pancras Hotel and the Ampthill Square Estate in Somers Town, Camden.

There is a café with toilets at the southern base of the hill.

Primrose Hill 119

Northala Fields from Northolt Church.

⑧

Hills Ancient and Modern

Perivale to Northolt

Very much a walk of two halves, this takes you from the ancient hill fort of Horsenden Hill, an unexpected slice of countryside surprisingly near the Central Line, to the very modern and artificial mounds of Northala Fields alongside the unpromising backdrop of the A40, separated by a pleasant meander along the towpath of the Grand Union Canal. The views from both eminences make the walk very worthwhile, and what the foothills of Northala Fields lack in altitude they certainly make up in arrestingly uninterrupted views both of central London's powerhouse skyline and of airliners suddenly and hair-raisingly dropping below the horizon to touch down at Heathrow.

Summits:
Horsenden Hill, 85m
Northala Fields, highest summit 22m

Length: 4 miles – 6.5 km
Time: 2 hours
Total ascent: 352 feet – 107 metres
Start: Perivale Station (Central Line)
Finish: Northolt Station (Central Line)
Base camp: Perivale Station has loos and a shop where you can buy snacks and drinks, but the immediate area is not blessed with coffee shops. The Horsenden Loaf is a pop-up café at Horsenden Farm visitor centre (public toilets here) advertised as opening Friday–Sunday, selling homemade cakes. The Black Horse pub is beside the Grand Union Canal, and there is a café at Northala Fields.

If you're taking the Central Line from the middle of London, remember to look out to the left on the approach to Perivale to see the Art Deco masterpiece of the Hoover Building, now a Tesco supermarket and flats.

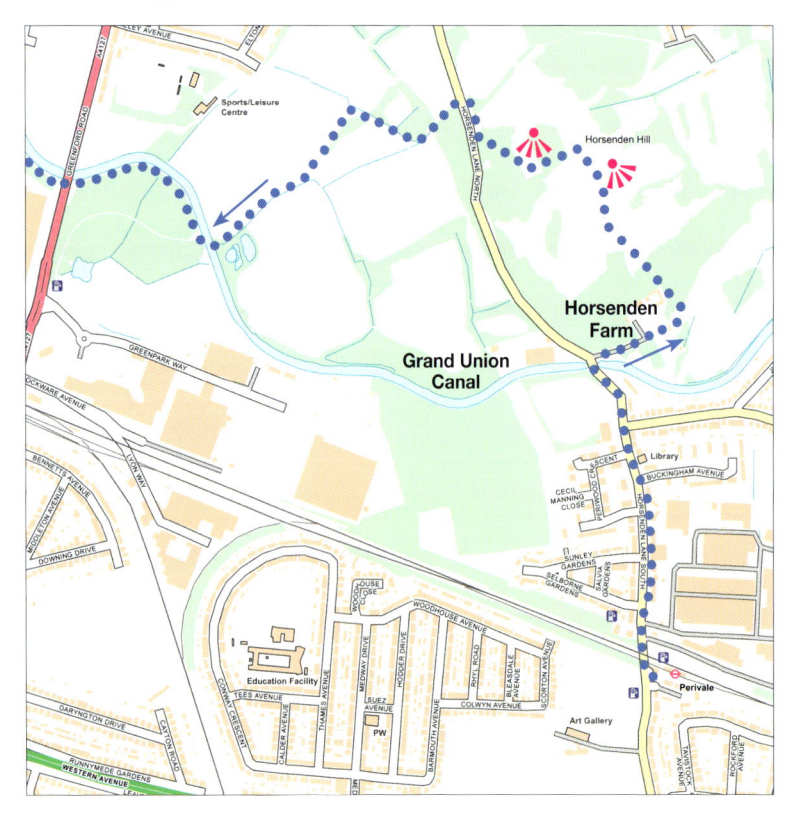

122 Hills Ancient and Modern

Turn right out of the station into Horsenden Lane South, which initially takes you through interwar housing but becomes progressively countrified. Cross the bridge over the Grand Union Canal and take the next road right, following signs to Horsenden Farm and Visitor Centre.

Just before the farmyard our route takes the path to the right. At the end of the farm buildings we start to climb straight away, following the Capital Ring signpost up a hedge-lined path away from the farm – go straight on; don't turn left. When you look back downhill you'll already be able to see out over the plain beyond the A40 and the sprawl of suburbia.

At a fork turn right and continue uphill. Just off to the right is a meadow offering a prospect of the City and the Battersea Power Station development to the left, and due south the Surrey Hills and North Downs. Continue up the steps ahead onto the edge of the Disc Golf and Foot course that is part of the Horsenden Hill Activity

Horsenden Farm

Horsenden Farm is an urban farm run as a community project by volunteers who grow vegetables and keep chickens. The produce is sold through the farm shop, open at weekends. Grouped around the farmyard outbuildings house other enterprises such as a brewery and a holistic gift and crystal shop, as well as toilet facilities. You'll find the Horsenden Loaf pop-up café on the approach road from Friday to Sunday.

Centre. Turn left to the grassy plateau that forms the top of Horsenden Hill, where among the tussocky grass you should see a trig point.

As you walk towards the trig point the panorama becomes more

The grassy terrace halfway up Horsenden Hill.

expansive. Wembley Arch (to the north) is immediately to your right. Looking south, you can already make out your destination: the four peaks of the Northala Hills, looking like prehistoric barrows, just behind where the A40 runs.

Carry on ahead to the grassy terrace,

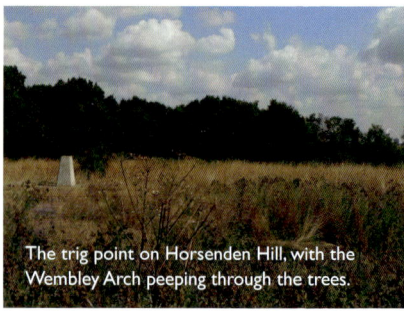

The trig point on Horsenden Hill, with the Wembley Arch peeping through the trees.

which covers an old underground reservoir. Here you can pick out more distant sights – there are some rather weather-beaten information boards to help with orientation. To the south-west is Windsor Castle (you might need some

The ascent from beside Horsenden Farm.

binoculars to spy this) and in the far west the Chiltern hills. Closer in, and to the north-east is Harrow-on-the-Hill, distinguished by the spire of the church above Harrow School.

From the terrace take the path heading downhill to your left (not the Capital Ring). As you descend, you'll see Harrow-on-the-Hill ahead of you. At the bottom of the hill is an apparently disused car park: turn left through it and out down the tarmac road. At the gate before the main road (Horsenden Lane North) follow the path to your right. Look out for a clearing in the hedge on your left, and cross the road carefully. Now take the footpath opposite signposted 'Berkeley Avenue'.

Once you're on the footpath ignore the

Horsenden Hill

Horsenden Hill is a precious nature reserve comprising 100 hectares of diverse habitats: woodland, wetland, meadows and farmland. The hill itself is a scheduled ancient monument, and archaeological excavations have revealed Neolithic, Bronze Age, Iron Age and Roman artifacts that suggest Horsenden has been farmed and occupied for millennia.

Over the past century the hill's eminent position has seen it put to many uses. During the First World War it was used as a gunnery position to repel Zeppelins, and in the Second World War it was a searchlight station to protect local factories. From the 1950s it was the site of a large but short-lived underground reservoir – you can still make out the rectangular patch of concrete.

Looking towards Northala Fields from the summit of Horsenden Hill.

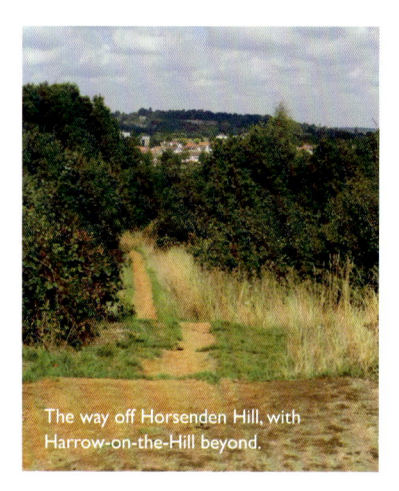

The way off Horsenden Hill, with Harrow-on-the-Hill beyond.

Grand Union Canal – Paddington Arm

The Grand Union Canal is an amalgamation of separate independent waterways that was finally completed early in the twentieth century to create a coherent artery for trade all the way between London and the Midlands. This stretch, named the Paddington Arm, was opened in 1801 and stretches 13 miles from the Paddington Basin to Hayes, where it joins another section of the Grand Union Canal going north.

first blue arrow, and follow the path to right. At the next blue arrow turn right. Exit the wood into an open field and follow the path along the edge of a field lined with oak trees. Look out for an opening on the right through the trees and cross a short bridge made out of old railway sleepers. Go straight across the next field and into Berkeley Fields sports ground – you should see rugby and football goalposts ahead of you.

Turn immediately left onto a sandy path skirting the edge of the playing fields in the direction of the Grand Union Canal. You should be able to see narrow boats peeping above the far edge of the field. Just before you reach the canal turn right and cross the bridge over to the south side of the canal. If you want to conclude your walk at this point, you can follow the signs towards Greenford Station which will plug you back into the Central Line. Otherwise follow the towpath in the direction signposted 'Uxbridge'.

A cormorant on the canal.

126 Hills Ancient and Modern

Horsenden Hill from the canal towpath.

As you walk along the tranquil corridor of the canal, where cyclists attempting to recreate the Tour de France are likely to be the major hazard, you'll now be able to appreciate the full, tree-covered bulk of Horsenden Hill beyond. Eventually you pass through the sizeable new residential development of Greenford Quay, and just beyond it you can, if you wish, detour up onto the road to find the Black Horse, a pub which serves food and has a canalside beer garden.

From here you continue along the unremarkable but pleasant enough tree-lined towpath for approximately another mile – amid the large industrial units on the left you might be able to spy the factory that makes the famous Brompton foldable bikes – until finally the Al Masjid ul Husseni mosque looms into sight on the opposite side of the canal.

Just beyond here, cross the bridge which takes you away from the canal, signposted 'Northolt'. Beyond the bridge the path takes you to the edge of Belvue Park. Turn left and walk along Bowdell Road adjacent to the park. The white church on the hill is St Mary's, Northolt – we'll visit it towards the end of the walk.

At the top of the road turn left into Kensington Road and follow it under the A40 road bridge. Almost immediately on your right is the entrance to Northala Fields.

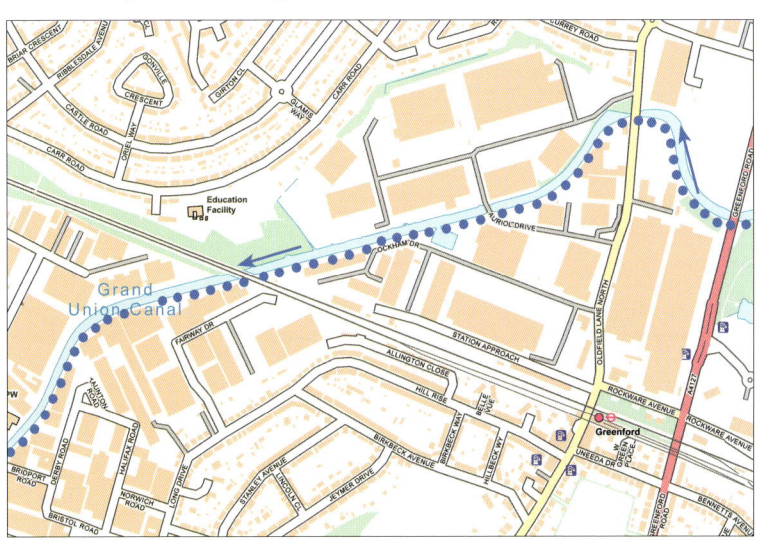

Perivale to Northolt 127

Northala Fields

Northala is the name for Northolt as recorded in the Domesday Book.

Opened in 2008 as part land art and part modern earthwork, this innovative development by Ealing Council alongside the A40 looks like nothing else in London. It's one of the most striking new landscapes anywhere in Greater London, and yet at the same time it also feels like coming upon a line of ancient tumuli.

Formerly these were playing fields, and the vision of transforming them into a twenty-first-century park was realised by the artist Peter Fink and the landscape architect Igor Marko. Four aligned hills were constructed using around 500,000 cubic metres of rubble from the demolition of the old Wembley Stadium and the redevelopment of White City shopping centre. Recycling on such a huge scale saw both projects reduce their carbon footprint substantially.

The hills and the surrounding park have been ingeniously devised to have multiple uses: to help combat noise and pollution from A40, create new habitats for wildlife, and be a focal point for community recreation and exercise. When I was there the birdlife was certainly living up to the hype: I spied a red kite, a meadow pipit and a couple of pied wagtails.

Make your way to the top of the second and tallest hill – the one with the beacon and circular path. These may be far from the highest eminences in London, but the 360° views are amazing: the whole of London is laid out before you, with information boards to help you with orientation and identifying the skyline. Highlights include:

- **to the north-east:** Harrow-on-the-Hill, Al Masjid ul Husseini mosque, Wembley Stadium, Horsenden Hill, Trellick Tower, the BT Tower, the Shard and the Aladdin Tower;
- **to the south-east:** Crystal Palace transmitter, the North Downs, Box Hill and the Gurdwara Sri Guru Singh Saba;
- **to the north-west**, the views stretch as far as the Chilterns, Oxhey Wood and Stanmore;
- **to the west:** you'll soon find yourself transfixed watching airliners swing in towards Heathrow on their final approach and descend with mesmerising momentum until they suddenly vanish below the houses and trees.

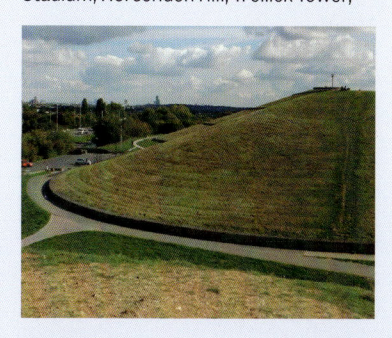

Perivale to Northolt

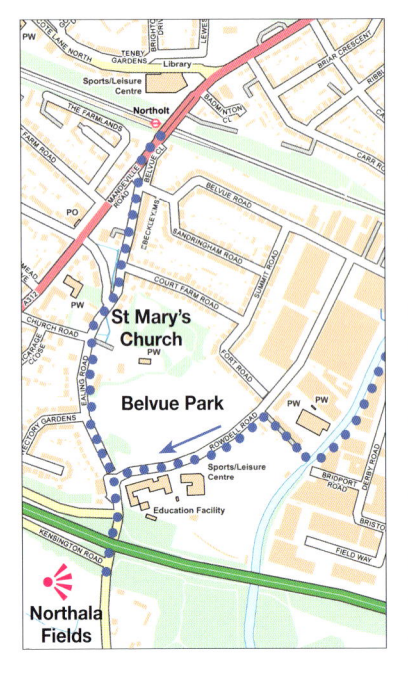

Having explored the hills, you'll find the café that looks out over the fishing lakes a convenient place for refreshments. It serves breakfast, light lunches, drinks and cakes, and there is a toilet there too.

Time to head for Northolt Station, which is approximately 20 minutes' walk. Just retrace your steps back along Kensington Road until the junction with Ealing Road. Continue along Ealing Road on the other side of Belvue Park and you will arrive in Northolt village. The small slice of rural idyll you'll find here is worth a quick detour and again makes the spectre of the A40 disappear. To the right, St Mary's Church, just off the attractive village green is one of London's smallest churches and dates back all the way to 1230. Beyond

Wembley Stadium

The new stadium with its stunning arch opened in 2007, and replaced the original Art Deco structure which had sat on the same site since 1923 and hosted England's endlessly celebrated 1966 World Cup Final victory as well as landmark rock concerts such as Live Aid.

The demolition of the Twin Towers at the old Wembley Stadium.

Designed by Populous and Foster and Partners, the new stadium's 133-metre-tall arch sits above the north stand and spans 315 metres, and can be seen from as far away as Croydon. It is the longest single span roof structure in the world, while the 90,000 seats make this the largest sports venue in the UK.

St Mary's Church, Northolt.

the churchyard is Belvue Park. Continue along Ealing Road and you will hit the junction with Mandeville Road. Keep right and you will see Northolt Station on the opposite side of road.

The village green below the church.

Perivale to Northolt 131

Stanmore Common, the path leading to the viewpoint.

9

Country and North-Western

Stanmore to Harrow Weald

This walk in the north-west reaches of Greater London takes you to the end of the Tube line, and then the end of suburbia, within minutes. In not many more minutes you're high up on Stanmore Hill taking in a fabulous prospect of the metropolis. The great views keep coming as our route keeps to the high ground through heathland commons and beech woods, taking in along the way a Second World War landmark and the erstwhile home of one of Britain's most celebrated lyricists.

Summits:
Stanmore, 152m – 4th highest point in London
Harrow Weald Common, 145m – 6th highest point in London
Old Redding, 137m

Length: 5 miles – 8 kilometres
Time: 3 hours
Total ascent: 349 feet –149 metres
Start: Stanmore Station – Jubilee Line
Finish: 182 bus from the Uxbridge Road, Harrow Weald to Harrow and Wealdstone Station (Overground), Harrow on-the-Hill (Metropolitan Line), Wembley Central (Bakerloo Line) or Wembley Park (Jubilee, Metropolitan Lines)
Base camp: Stanmore town centre (ten minutes' walk from the station) at the start. Two rather smart options near the end: the Grim's Dyke Hotel and the Hare at Old Redding.

From Stanmore Station cross the road into Kerry Court, which in turn leads to Kerry Avenue, lined with entrancing white Art Deco villas. Continue up the road until it gives out at the entrance to Stanmore Country Park. Mere minutes from the

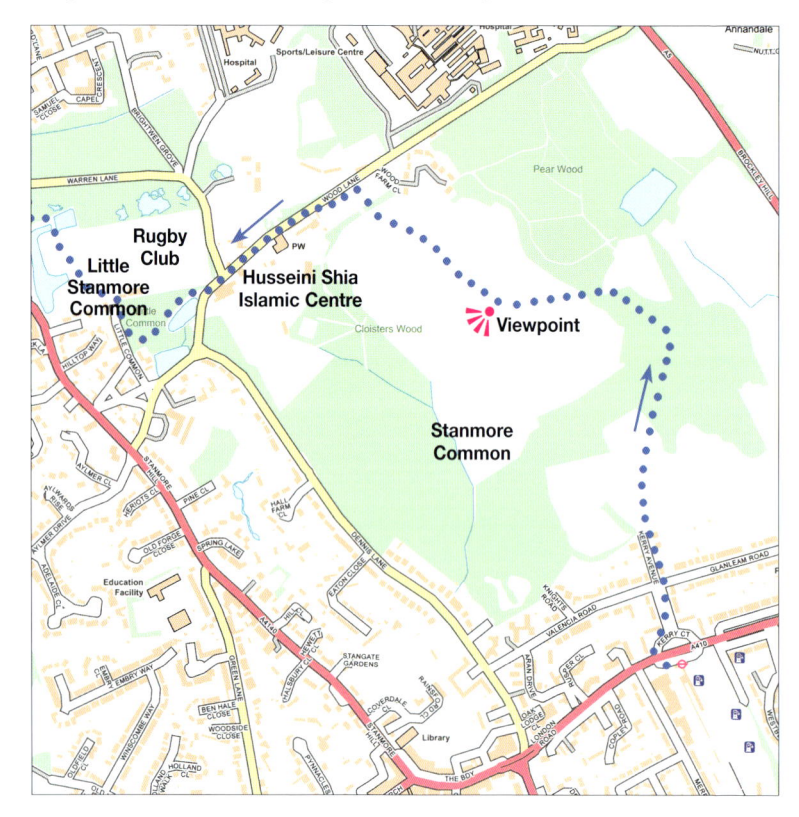

The Art Deco houses in Kerry Avenue.

The path up through Stanmore Country Park.

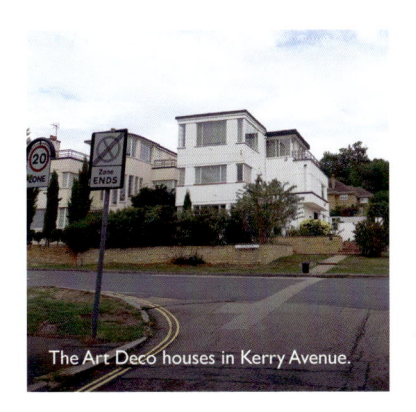

end of the Tube line and already you find yourself in woodland – though the distant murmur of the M1 slightly disturbs the peace and tranquillity.

Head straight on at the signpost and then take the right-hand fork (not the London Loop). Continue through the woods and across the clearing. At the junction in the path keep straight on through more woodland until you come out into scrubland amid newly planted trees. This is Woods Farm, recently added to the area of open space. Turn right at the sign that points towards 'London Viewpoint'. From this plateau the most spectacular view of London will unfold, and when you reach the viewpoint you'll find an information board to point it all out for you.

• To the west is Harrow-on-the-Hill, the church of St Mary's and, slightly to its left, Horsenden Hill;

• in the foreground is the Wembley Arch; behind it, the North Downs and Surrey Hills;

Stanmore to Harrow Weald 135

The London skyline from the viewpoint.

• it's also possible to pick out Trellick Tower, the Crystal Palace and Croydon transmitter masts, the Strata building at Elephant and Castle (the so-called 'Electric Razor', with its wind turbines that don't turn), St George's Tower and the Nine Elms development, and the BT Tower;

• to the left (east), you can see the prominent ridge of Hampstead and Highgate, with the Shard, City and Docklands skyline peeking out behind;

• further on round to the east, St James's Church at Muswell Hill and Alexandra Palace are also visible.

It's also, it was immediately evident when I came up here, a wonderful place for flying a kite.

Having drunk in the view, follow the signpost to Wood Lane, which brings you to a gravel path signposted 'Wood Farm Car Park'. Exit onto Wood Lane (a busy road) and follow the pavement to the left until you come to Husseini Shia Islamic Centre.

This Grade II-listed building, now rescued from a perilous state of dilapidation, was originally named Warren House and built in the late eighteenth century by the Duke of Chandos as part of his estate. It is thought the Warren House estate occupied the site of what had been the Roman town of Sulloniacae.

The path across Wood Farm.

More recently the building was known as Springbok House and home to a geriatric hospital originally funded by the South African government to commemorate the country's Second World War dead. Here you must carefully cross the road towards Warren Lane.

Once the road is crossed, ignore Warren Lane and instead follow a path on your left that heads into woodland. This will lead you around the back of the back of a rugby ground which constitutes the highest point on Stanmore Hill.

Now follow the London Loop sign, and you'll find the path emerging onto what appears to be a village green. This is the hamlet of Little Stanmore Common. Cross the common and aim for the wooded area beyond the houses. The London Loop, signposted again, takes you behind the houses until you reach a pond. Turn right here and follow the path between two ponds.

These are known as Lower and Upper Spring Ponds, are possibly man-made and certainly date back at least to Roman times and Sulloniacae. Upper Spring Pond is also known locally as Caesar's Pond, so you never know. Look out for the electric blue flash of a kingfisher here – I spotted one.

The path leads you along the side of Stanmore Cricket Club and out through its car park. Cross the road and follow the London Loop path opposite into the trees. At the tarmac path go straight on and follow a path into the Warren Lane car park of Stanmore Common. Our walk does not include Stanmore Common, but if you want to take a look, there is a an information board map in the car park that maps the paths around it.

Our walk leaves the car park and turns

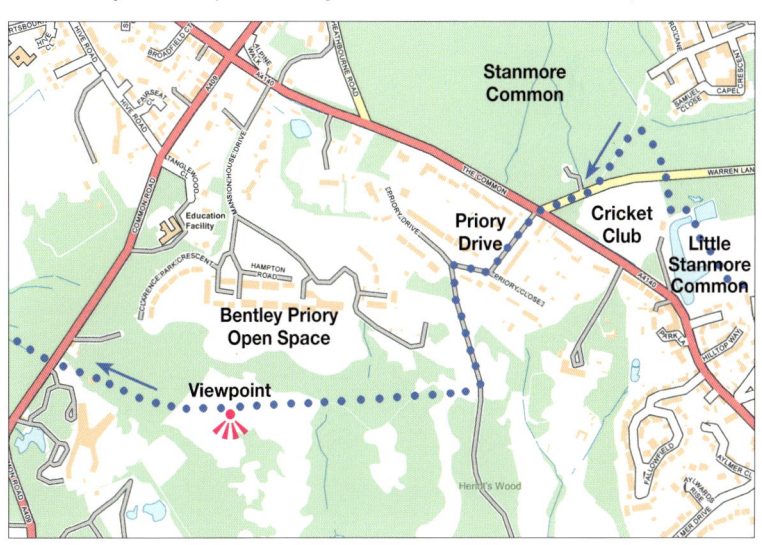

Bentley Priory

The name is taken from a twelfth-century Augustine priory that originally stood on the land. In 1766, the priory was knocked down and replaced by a large house at the highest point on the ridge.

Two decades later the estate was sold to the 9th Earl of Abercorn, who appointed the eminent architect Sir John Soane, of Bank of England and eponymous museum fame, to extend and refurbish the house. Since then, the house has had a lively history. It was the final home of the Dowager Queen Adelaide, the wife of William IV, until her death in 1849, and then a hotel and a girls' school before being acquired in 1926 by the Royal Air Force.

It was its role in the Second World War that sealed Bentley Priory's place in posterity, as the HQ of RAF Fighter Command. During the Battle of Britain

Fighter Command's Operations Room.

An aerial view of Bentley Priory in 1944.

in 1940 it was the nerve centre of the RAF's entire defence effort under Fighter Command's Commander-in-Chief Hugh Dowding. In Bentley Priory's Operations Room, on a daily, often hour-by-hour basis, female croupiers would move markers on a huge map of the south-east of England to show German air raids, and the RAF's available resources of Spitfire and Hurricane squadrons, for Dowding and his group commanders to deploy to engage them. If the Battle of Britain was won in the air, then the victory was planned on the ground, and not least at Bentley Priory.

The mansion remained in RAF hands until 2008 and, while the estate is now an extensive residential development, part of the building was opened as a museum in 2013 dedicated to its RAF heritage.

If you want to visit the museum (opening times bentleypriorymuseum.org.uk), then, instead of turning into Priory Drive, turn right and continue along Common Road until you find the entrance to the Bentley Priory Estate on your left, from where you'll be signposted to the museum's main entrance.

Following your visit there are no short-cuts back into Bentley Priory Open Space and you will have to retrace your steps to Priory Drive. To finish the walk here you can catch the 142 bus on Common Road back to Stanmore Tube station.

left onto Warren Lane towards the road ahead. Cross the road (The Common) and follow a sign to Bentley Priory Open Space. This takes you along Priory Drive, a private road with many opulent villas. Turn right at the road junction and then then left onto a footpath which leads into the Bentley Priory Open Space and Bentley Nature Reserve.

Turn right onto the path that leads towards Harrow Weald Common and Old Redding, and through the gate into Spring Meadow. On the right through the trees you'll see Bentley Priory house. Bentley Nature Reserve slopes southwards down from Bentley Priory, and includes two bodies of water, Summerhouse Lake and Boot Pond, Heriot Wood and a small herd of fallow deer.

At the top of the concrete path a bench offers a viewpoint commanding more fine views out over London. Through binoculars we were even able to pick out Westminster Abbey.

The path takes you to a gate, beyond which it continues uphill out of the nature reserve and onto Common Road. Cross the road and take the steps immediately opposite down into Harrow Weald Common. This is the highest point of the walk.

Carry straight on, following the waymarking of the London Loop path through attractive beech woods. At the edge of the woods you'll come upon a set of substantial gates. Take the path to your left through the trees. At path marker 17 take the right fork and continue on it until you reach a road. Turning left along the road will bring you to the Grim's Dyke Hotel, which is worth a look, and not overly grand or stuffy. During the warmer months the terrace overlooking the beautiful gardens is a particularly lovely place for a pit stop.

You now have a choice in route. If you're visiting the hotel, you can see Grim's Dyke by exiting through its grounds (route A). Otherwise, follow route B.

A) Via hotel

At the far end of the garden take the steps up and follow the path to the left, past the majestic redwood trees, until you reach the pond.

B) If not visiting hotel

Take the path immediately to the left before the Hotel sign and road entrance.

Grim's Dyke House/Hotel

Built in 1870, the house was designed by the renowned Victorian architect Norman Shaw in a style mixing Gothic Revival with late Elizabethan for the artist Frederick Goodall. In 1890 it was bought by Sir W. S. Gilbert, the well-known librettist of Gilbert and Sullivan fame, who lived there until his death in 1911. Gilbert died of a heart attack attempting to save a young woman guest who had got into trouble swimming in one of the many ponds within the grounds. Subsequently the house became a recuperation facility for TB patients before conversion into a hotel.

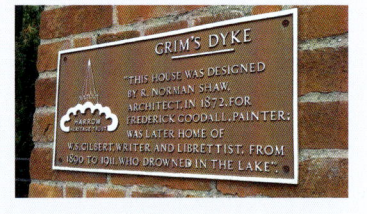

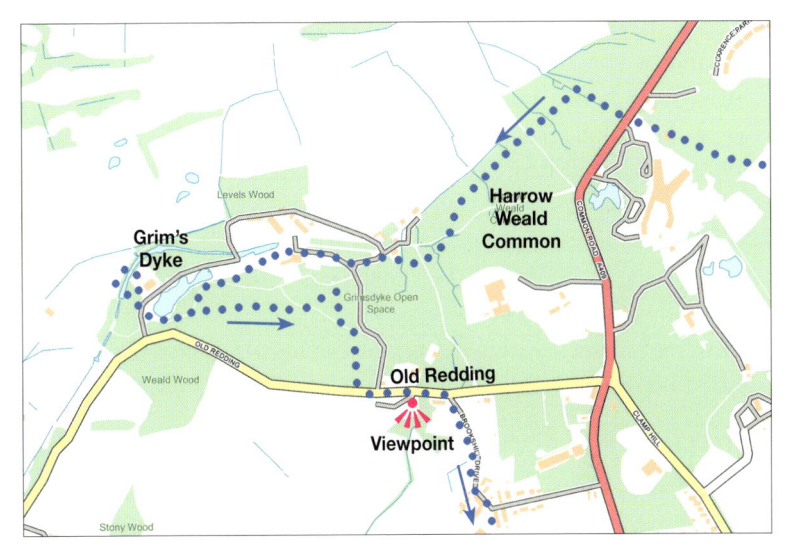

Follow the path around the perimeter of hotel grounds until you find yourself at the end of the hotel garden. Take the path to the left and you'll find yourself at the pond.

The path hugs the left-hand side of the pond: look out for London Loop signs. Cross a small road (which leads to a telecommunications station) onto a wooded path. Turn left into the woods; there is a pond to your right. On this path you'll find Grim's Dyke is now on your right – it's pretty atmospheric. At the end of the path you drop down onto a lane. Immediately opposite is an explanatory stone marker for Grim's Dyke.

Now retrace your steps back to the garden pond, but then instead of heading back to the hotel, take the path uphill to your right and keep going up to the road, Old Redding.

Cross the road carefully and go through the car park to the viewpoint. Once again, here are amazing views: across to Harrow-on-the-Hill and, in the distance, the North Downs and Surrey Hills. If you have binoculars, then to the west you can see Heathrow Airport.

After you've enjoyed the view, make your way to the exit at the east of the car park. Turn right onto a path which passes a pub, the Case is Altered, which at the time of writing was closed. A little further in the same direction you'll come upon another hostelry, the Hare at Old Redding, something of a foodie destination, and not somewhere you should expect basic pub grub. At busy times you might need to book ahead.

Follow the path along Old Redding until you see the sign 'Footpath 29 and 30'. This path takes you around Copse Farm, and

Stanmore to Harrow Weald 141

The view from Old Redding.

Footpath 29 and 30

Copse Farm

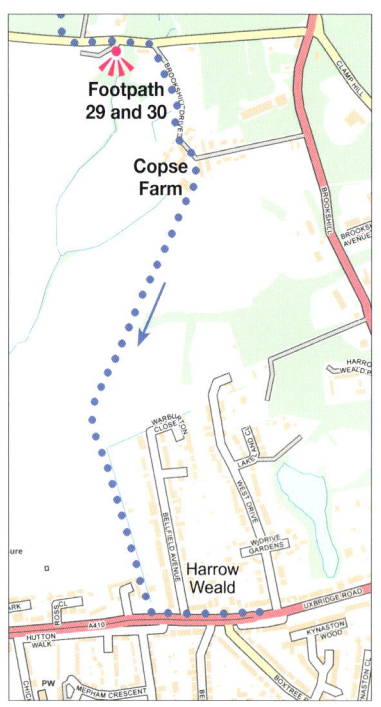

Harrow Weald

then heads downhill with wonderful and unexpected countryside views to the right. After about half a mile the surroundings become a little more urban, and the path runs between two sports grounds. At

the end of the path is the Uxbridge Road. Turn left and in 100 metres is a stop for the 182 bus, which will connect you with the following Tube and railway stations: Harrow and Wealdstone, Harrow-on-the-Hill, Wembley Central and Wembley Park.

A section of Grim's Dyke beyond the hotel.

The descent from Old Redding.

Trig Points

Properly named triangulation points, these triangular concrete pillars that pepper the landscape were part of the Ordnance Survey's Retriangulation project, which commenced in 1935. Its aim was to re-survey Britain and, in the process, create a unified, nationwide network for mapping using triangulation data collected between these designated trig points.

The original triangulation of Britain had begun in 1782, when the Royal Society supported the assertion of Major-General William Roy that accurate maps were a military necessity. Using advancements in science and mathematic formulae, Roy established what would become the basis of all modern surveying: triangulation. Above all, the mapping of Britain using this new method led to the formation of the Ordnance Survey in 1791, the year after Roy's death.

The new pillars were built to a design by Brigadier Martin Hotine, the head of the Retriangulation project. They feature a level platform for a theodolite, providing a fixed surveying station and thereby improving the accuracy of the readings

Triangulation

Triangulation is an exercise in trigonometry (hence the colloquial name for triangulation pillars), and a method of determining the location of a point by reference to two other known points.

If you measure the angles to it from these two points, then the point must lie where those two angular axes intersect: in other words, at the third point of the triangle. For mapping a whole area, you establish a baseline on a grid, measure the angle of every third point from both ends, and eventually a network of interlocking triangles will pinpoint the location of everywhere on the grid.

Pole Hill.

Horsenden Hill.

obtained. Between 1936 and 1962 6,500 of these trig points were built.

Because line of sight was a key requirement, pillars tended to be built on high ground, but this is not always the case. For example, the highest trig point in the UK is indeed at the top of Ben Nevis, but the lowest is at Little Ouse in the Fens, at 1 metre below sea level.

The march of technology has since rendered trig points obsolete, as surveyors now use the OS Net network of 110 Global Navigation Satellite System (GNSS) receivers to accurately plot new map details. Approximately 6,000 of these trig points remain (no one knows for sure) as artefacts from another age.

Surprisingly, however, there are only 24 trig points in London, according to the meticulous blogger Diamond Geezer. A number of them are well hidden on

Hilly Fields.

private land or overgrown, but we do visit a few on our walks – Horsenden Hill, Hilly Fields and Pole Hill.

These days 'trig-bagging' or 'trig-pointing' has become a popular hobby, as 'collectors' travel the country spotting and recording as many as possible.

Trig Points 145

The wisteria in full bloom on the Pergola in the Hill Garden above Golders Hill Park.

⑩

High on the Heath

Hampstead Heath to Golders Green

No walking guide to the heights of London could omit Hampstead Heath, one of the most glorious of the capital's green spaces, and such well-known landmarks as Parliament Hill and Kenwood House. This walk visits both, on an undulating route traversing the heath that gradually climbs to one of the highest points anywhere in London. But it continues to take in lesser-known gems beyond, such as North End, the Hill Garden Pergola and Golders Hill Park. Virtually the entire walk is through woods or on rolling grassland, and there are justifiably famous views out across London.

Summits:
Parliament Hill, 98m
Kenwood House, 134m
Hampstead Heath west of Spaniards Way, 137m
– joint 9th highest point in London
Golders Hill Park, 112m

Length: 4 miles – 6.5 kilometres
Time: 2½ hours
Total ascent: 609 feet – 186 metres
Start: Hampstead Heath Station (Overground)
Finish: Golders Green Station (Northern Line)
Base camp: South End Road opposite Hampstead Heath Station; Kenwood House, Golders Hill Park (toilets at both too). As you'd expect in this deliciously well-heeled part of London there are plenty of spots for refreshments. There are also public toilets at various other signposted points on the heath.

As you come out of Hampstead Heath Station you are at the junction of South Hill Park Road and South End Road. To your right on South Hill Park Road is the Magdala pub – forever to be associated with Ruth Ellis, the last woman to be executed in England. It was outside this pub that she shot her lover. Nowadays it's a popular place for food and drink. On the far side of South End Road there is a wealth of cafés and eateries, as well as a branch of Daunt Books.

The start of the walk is the Hampstead Heath map information board, which you'll

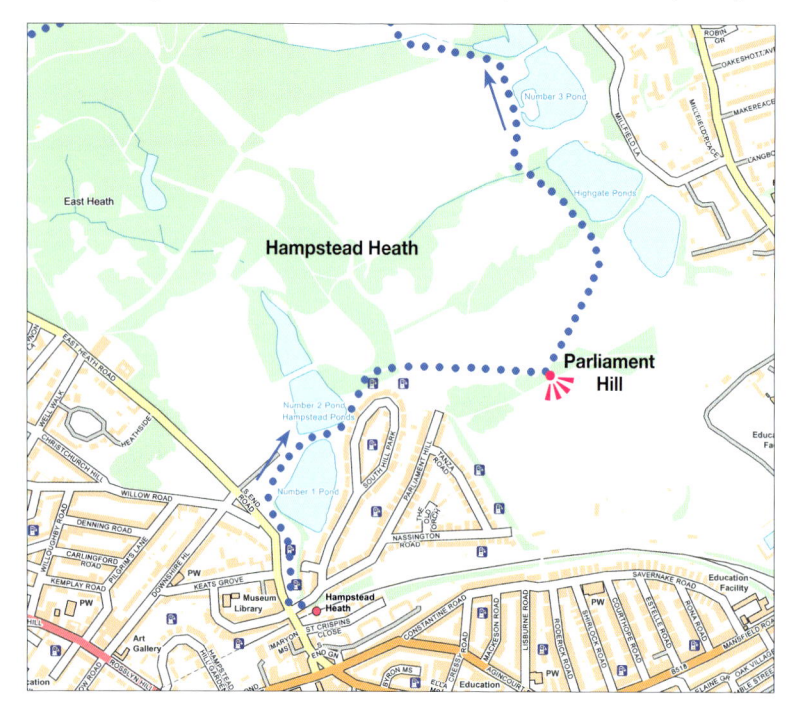

148 High on the Heath

Hampstead Heath

The 800 acres of rambling, hilly and verdant Hampstead Heath, which now includes Parliament Hill, Golders Hill, Kenwood and other pockets of land, have been preserved for the public thanks to determined campaigns over the past 150 years.

Originally the heath was a smaller area of common land that dated back to the Saxon manor of Hampstead and as such its citizens had rights to graze cattle, gather wood and dig for sand. As London expanded, the attractions of the Heath became well known, both commercially and recreationally.

In the seventeenth century the Hampstead Water Company began creating reservoirs from diverted brooks (see Lost Rivers), sand extraction was a local industry, and between 1808 and 1814 the naval telegraph shutter system was located on Hampstead Heath, connecting the Admiralty in London with the naval port at Great Yarmouth. In the eighteenth century Hampstead and the heath gained a reputation as a spa and, after the arrival of the railway (what is now the Overground), a day-tripper destination.

All this led to the now fashionable village of Hampstead increasingly encroaching on the heathland. The tipping point was an attempt by the incumbent Lord of the Manor, Sir Thomas Maryon Wilson, to build on it, which was subsequently blocked by the courts and prompted the Hampstead Heath Act of 1871, to protect it for public use.

Subsequent threats to adjacent land led to the intervention of the Common Protection Society, and the renowned housing reformer (and founder of the National Trust) Octavia Hill. Funds were raised for the public purchase of more land, and 1888 saw the Hampstead Heath Extension Act.

find on the station side of South End Road. From here take the path uphill onto the heath. Follow the path to the right past the pond to go across the second bridge on the right. The mixed swimming pond, one of the heath's three famous bathing ponds, is on your left.

The path continues ahead uphill through the woods. At the fork take path to the right, and keep going uphill until you come out onto greensward. Head to the top: this is Parliament Hill, our first summit, and one of London's most famous eminences.

Now we head downhill again, eastwards, towards the pond. When you

The Lost River Fleet and Hampstead Heath's Ponds

The River Fleet is one of the lost rivers of London, nowadays hidden away in the sewers of north London and the City until it reaches the Thames at Blackfriars. But its source is the twin brooks that flow on either side of the heath, which eventually join to form the Fleet somewhere underneath Kentish Town.

The Hampstead Brook, on the western side, starts in the Vale of Health Pond: here, in the undergrowth, is the only place where you can actually see the River Fleet in any form. In the seventeenth century the brook was dammed to create the three Hampstead Ponds. Originally these served as reservoirs for drinking water; they have since been repurposed, one as the mixed bathing pond.

The Highgate Brook, on the eastern side, rises within the Kenwood Estate. It too was dammed, to create the eight Highgate Ponds, dug in their present form between 1690 and 1740 as reservoirs for drinking water, and still supplying London into the nineteenth century. These days the ponds include the single-sex male and female swimming ponds and the Model Boating Pond.

The Model Boating Pond.

Parliament Hill

Originally part of Tottenhall Manor dating back to the twelfth century, Parliament Hill is said to have got its name during the English Civil War when it was occupied by soldiers loyal to Parliament. The hill remained private property until the late nineteenth century, when it was purchased for the public and incorporated into Hampstead Heath.

It remains one of the finest viewpoints in London. To the south there are views of the City and St Paul's Cathedral, the Shard, Canary Wharf and Docklands. You'll also be able to make out the Strata building at Elephant & Castle ('the Electric Razor', with its permanently becalmed wind turbines in the roof), and the BT Tower. In the distance are the hills of south-east London, including Shooters Hill and Crystal Palace with its transmitter mast. Closer in is the Caledonian Park Clock Tower, the last relic of the Metropolitan Cattle Market that opened in 1855 and closed in the 1960s.

To the east you'll see Highgate's churches, notably the spire of St Michael's Church (the highest church above sea level in London), and the green cupola of St Joseph's Church. To the west is St John's Church in Hampstead.

reach it, take the path to the left. For the rest of our ascent of the heath always keep the Highgate Ponds on your right.

At a fork in the path bear right, and we begin climbing again, up the gentle

The path off Parliament Hill towards the Model Boating Pond.

slope ahead. Pass the Model Boating Pond, and at the railings turn left. Continue on uphill with another pond to your right. The path then divides into three: carry straight on through the wood, with views across to Highgate on your right. The gate ahead takes you into the Kenwood Estate. Whereas Hampstead Heath itself is managed by the City of London, the Kenwood Estate is run by English Heritage; seasonal closing times are posted on all the gates.

Continue ahead through the woods, which in the spring are awash with bluebells. Now the pale edifice of Kenwood House appears ahead of you, while to your left is a lake and an ornamental bridge. It's now a pleasant walk up the grassy slope to the house on its terrace, and our second summit.

After exploring the delights of Kenwood, follow the main path across the terrace to the west of the house, along the impressive avenue of lime trees, and just beyond you'll see some reclining figures by Henry Moore. Take the path to

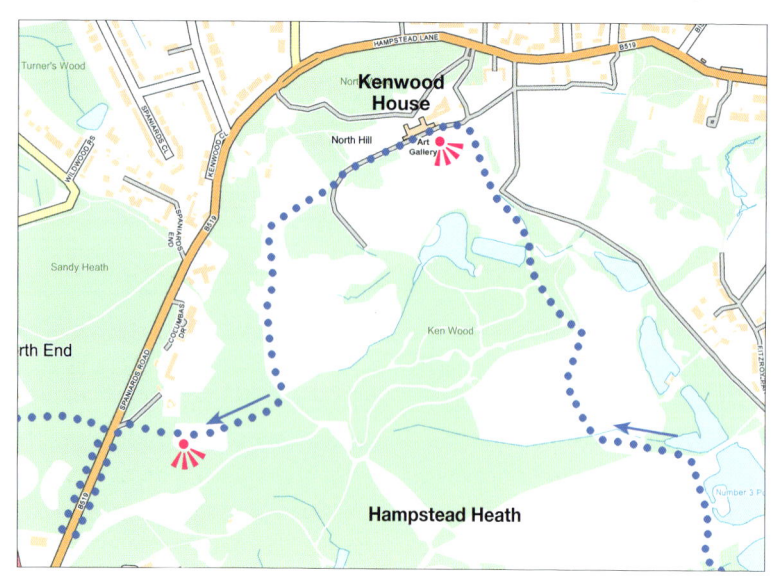

Kenwood House

Kenwood House enjoys a prominent hilltop setting, with a spectacular parkland vista designed by the doyen of landscape, Sir Humphry Repton. Depending upon the time of year and the tree cover, views of the distant City and St Paul's emerge.

The house itself is a Palladian masterpiece created by the renowned architect Robert Adam, after the 1st Earl of Mansfield had purchased the estate in 1754. In 1922 the house and its contents were auctioned. Kenwood's saviour was Edward Guinness, the 1st Earl of Iveagh, who bought the house and 74 acres of surrounding land. Upon his death the Iveagh Bequest Act of 1929 stipulated that Kenwood and its contents should be open to the public, free of charge.

Lord Iveagh's superb art collection, with key works by Rembrandt, Gainsborough and Vermeer, to mention but a few, was also to remain with the house, and is on view there today. There is a also café with indoor and outdoor seating and a lovely formal garden. You can easily spend a couple of hours here.

the left, which heads downwards into the woods. Near here, and at least one other site on the heath, is where the Express Dairy, which used to run the café at Kenwood, dumped all its broken crockery. Monogrammed shards can still be unearthed. Leave the Kenwood enclosure through the gate.

Turn right, left, and right again to follow the middle path heading to the right through the wood. Now you'll find yourself gently climbing again, and notice a large fallen tree on your left. The path takes you down into the valley, and then uphill again

Central London beyond the Vale of Health from the top of the heath.

to emerge into a large, grassy, open space. Continue straight ahead until you see a gate marked 'Exit'. It was here that Sir Thomas Maryon Wilson proposed to build his doomed 28-villa development named East Park.

Just before it, however, look out to your left for a viewpoint with a seat under the trees that offers fabulous views across the Vale of Health (the small development down in the dip) all the way to the skyline of Canary Wharf and Docklands. This is taken to be the highest point on Hampstead Heath, and is definitely a place to halt a moment.

Leave the heath by the gate to come out on Spaniards Road. Don't try to cross the busy road here, but turn left and use

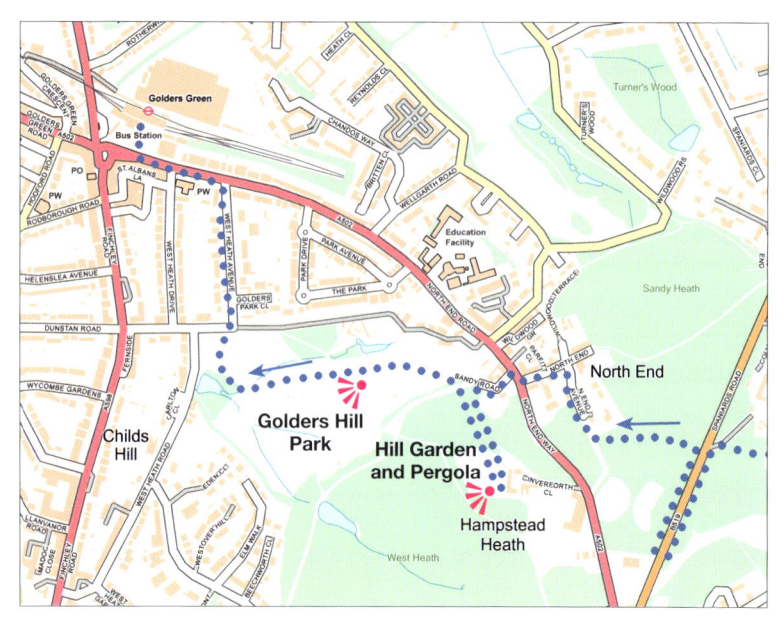

154 High on the Heath

the pedestrian crossing near Jack Straw's Castle, a former pub and local landmark now converted for residential use.

Once we've crossed the road we turn right to follow the path back along the

The West Heath.

road on the opposite side. Pass the exit gate we came out of and, approximately 100 metres further on your left, you'll see a 'Hampstead Heath' sign and a path into the woods. Enter here and continue straight along the path.

That these woods dip below the road is not down to the natural topography. In the nineteenth century this was the site of sand excavation on an industrial scale, owing to the fine Bagshot sand deposited bounteously upon the ridge during the Eocene period – in 1813 it was estimated that the heath was covered to an average depth with 10 feet of sand. Always one to exploit for his own gain, Sir Thomas Maryon Wilson (him again) leased extraction rights to the Midland Railway Company, who used the sand to lay the main line to St Pancras. Exploitation of the heath's resources came to an end with public ownership.

Maintain a downhill course through the woods, and eventually you'll come out on a quiet residential road with a faintly rural character. This is the hamlet of North End. On the left a plaque asserts that William Pitt the Elder, a former prime minister, lived here between 1708 and 1778.

At the crossroads, the road to the right leads back into the heath, but this walk turns to the left past Hogarth Court. At the junction with North End Road is the Old Bull and Bush pub, immortalised in a music hall song made famous by Florrie Forde in 1904. A drinking house, previously frequented by Hogarth and others, has apparently been on this site for centuries, though the existing pub only dates from the 1880s.

An invisible, indeed phantom, landmark close to the Old Bull and Bush

The ghostly North End Station far beneath the Old Bull and Bush.

Hampstead Heath to Golders Green 155

Hill Garden and Pergola

The Pergola is probably not as a big a secret as it once was – at peak times you have to dodge the wedding photographers and TikTok artists – but it is truly worth exploring, especially in late spring and early summer when the wisteria and roses are in their prime.

It was built by Lord Leverhulme as part of the garden of the extravagant mansion Hill House above (now called Inverforth House and converted into the inevitable apartments), and really does embody the opulent spirit of the Edwardian age. After Leverhulme's death in 1925 the gardens fell into disrepair, and it is only in recent times that they are gradually being fully restored.

From the look-out there are great views across to the west of Harrow-on-the-Hill and, in the nearer distance, the spire of St Mary's Church, Hampstead.

Lord Leverhulme

Lord Leverhulme founded the conglomerate Lever Brothers, and made his fortune from, among other things, Sunlight Soap. His other extravagant projects included the model industrial village of Port Sunlight on Merseyside to house his factory workers, and a thoroughly unsuccessful attempt to found the new town of Leverburgh on the island of Harris in the Outer Hebrides.

is one of London's ghost Tube stations, the uncompleted North End Station, which would have sat on the Northern line between Hampstead and Golders Green and at 67 metres been the deepest station below ground on the network. Construction was abandoned in 1906 as local opposition scuppered the property development it would have served, and the land was instead purchased to enlarge the heath. However, the subterranean station did subsequently play a secret role in Cold War defence, when a floodgate control room was built to help prevent the flooding of central London Underground stations in the event of a nuclear attack.

At the Old Bull and Bush cross the road into Sandy Road immediately opposite. Follow Sandy Road round into a wooded area known as the West Heath. After a few metres you'll see the entrance to Golders Hill Park on your right. We will be going to the park, but not yet. Instead, almost opposite and on your left are steps leading in the opposite direction. Follow these and take path to the left, which climbs uphill. Ahead of you is the gate for the Hill Garden and Pergola.

At the top of the park used to be Golders Hill House, last owned by Sir Thomas Spencer Wells, surgeon to Queen Victoria's household. Upon his death the Victorian mansion and grounds were saved from more rapacious developers by yet another soap baron, Thomas Barratt, Chairman of A. & F. Pears, manufacturers of Pears soap. The philanthropic Barratt duly made the house and grounds over to the London County Council, and they were incorporated into Hampstead Heath and opened as Golders Hill Park in 1898. The house was destroyed by a parachute mine during the Second World War.

Golders Hill Park is lush, green and

The café in Golders Hill Park, from among the rhododendrons.

pleasantly undulating, not surprising as it was landscaped in the eighteenth century by Sir Humphry Repton. These days it boasts formal gardens, a deer enclosure, a children's play area and zoo, and is a very popular local destination. The terrace at the top is the last viewpoint on our walk, with further views above the trees of the hills around Harrow-on-the-Hill. The café here is a good place for a pit stop.

Continue downhill past the zoo, and follow a path that keeps the pond on your left and the tennis courts on your right. Leave the park through the gate onto West Heath Road. Turn right and then left into West Heath Avenue, and then left again into North End Road. Continue downhill to the junction with Finchley Road. Turn right and follow the road to Golders Green Station, for the Northern Line.

The top of Golders Hill Park, looking west.

Bibliography and Useful Web Addresses

Further walking guides
The Capital Ring by Colin Saunders (Aurum, 2020)
The London Loop by Colin Saunders (Aurum, 2017)
The Vanguard Way by Colin Saunders (1997)
London Tree Walks by Paul Wood (Safe Haven, 2020)
Green Chain Walk: tfl.gov.uk/modes/walking/green-chain-walk
Tandridge Border Path: walkingpages.co.uk
Thomas England Walk: friendsofraphaelpark.org.uk
Grand Union Canal Walk: canalrivertrust.org.uk
London M25 Master (Collins, 2003)

General London websites
The Londonist: londonist.com (especially for Hampstead rivers)
Diamond Geezer blog (especially for trig points)
Ordnance Survey: ordnance survey.co.uk (also for trig points)
londongeopartnership.org.uk (for London geology)
London Natural History Society: lnhs.org.uk
hidden-london.com
british-history.ac.uk
royalparks.org.uk

Alexandra Palace to Archway
highgate cemetery.org
parkland-walk.org.uk
alexandrapalace.com
Highgate Woods - haringey.gov.uk
Friends of Queens Wood: fqw.org.uk
waterlowpark.org.uk

Chingford and the Sewardstone Hills
visiteppingforest.org
Epping Forest Heritage Trust: efht.org.uk
T. E. Lawrence Society: telsociety.org.uk
Sewardstone Park Cemetery: spcemetery.com
Gillwell Park, Scout Association: scoutadventures.org.uk

Romford to Havering Park
Lodge Farm Park model railway: rideonrailways.co.uk/hmrc
friendsofraphaelpark.org.uk
Essex Wildlife Trust: essexwt.org.uk
havering.gov.uk

Brockley to Greenwich
streettreesforliving.org
Friends of Hilly Fields: hilly.org.uk
blackheath.org
The Ranger's House: english-heritage.org.uk
friendsofgreenwichpark.org.uk
Royal Museums Greenwich: rmg.co.uk

Old Royal Naval College: Greenwich ornc.org

New Cross Gate to Forest Hill
Friends of Telegraph Hill: thehill.org.uk/society/history
Friends of Nunhead Cemetery: fonc.org.uk
Horniman Museum: horniman.ac.uk
The Wood That Built London by C. J. Schuler (Sandstone Press, 2021)

Crystal Palace
crystalpaleparktrust.org
The Story of Gardening by Penelope Hobhouse (Dorling Kindersley, 2002)
crystalpalacefoundation.org.uk

East Croydon to New Addington
Croydon.gov.uk
friendsofselsdonwood.co.uk
parkhillpark.org.uk
Croydon Ecology Centre
Friends of Littleheath Woods: folw.co.uk
Croydoncentralparks (blog)
Concretopia: A Journey Around the Rebuilding of Post-war Britain by John Grindrod (Old Street, 2014)

Richmond to Wimbledon
parksandgardens.org
visitrichmond.co.uk
richmondsociety.org.uk
Wimbledon and Putney Commons: wpcc.org.uk
Skyline London by Caroline Dale (Aurum, 2012)

Guinness Hills
The Garden in the Machine by Tim Strangleman (OUP, 2019)

Perivale to Northolt
horsenden.co.uk
ealing.gov.uk
canalrivertrust.org.uk

Stanmore to Old Redding
stanmoretouristboard.org.uk
Bentleypriorymuseum.org.uk
grimsdyke.com/history

Hampstead Heath to Golders Green
Hampstead Heath: The Walker's Guide by David McDowall and Deborah Wolton (David McDowall, 2021)
hampsteadheath.net
London's Lost Rivers by Tom Bolton (Strange Attractor Press, 2020)
Kenwood: www.english-heritage.org.uk/visit/places/kenwood/
North End Station: ltmuseum.co.uk